NURSING AND HEALTH-CARE
RESEARCH

A Practical Guide
Second Edition

NURSING AND HEALTH-CARE RESEARCH

A Practical Guide

Second Edition

The Use and Application of Research for Nurses and other Health Care Professionals

WENDY COUCHMAN MSc BA CSS
*Professor and Head of School of
Education and Health Studies,
South Bank University, London*

JANE DAWSON MSc PhD SRN HV
*Clinical Audit Facilitator,
Portsmouth Hospitals Trust*

Baillière Tindall

PUBLISHED IN ASSOCIATION WITH THE RCN

London   Philadelphia   Toronto   Sydney   Tokyo

Baillière Tindall   24–28 Oval Road
London NW1 7DX

The Curtis Center
Independence Square West
Philadelphia, PA 19106–3399, USA

Harcourt Brace & Company
55 Horner Avenue
Toronto, Ontario M8Z 4X6, Canada

Harcourt Brace & Company, Australia
30–52 Smidmore Street
Marrickville
NSW 2204, Australia

Harcourt Brace & Company, Japan
Ichibancho Central Building
22-1 Ichibancho
Chiyoda-ku, Tokyo 102, Japan

A catalogue record for this book is available from the British Library

ISBN 1-873853-28-9

Printed and bound in Great Britain by WBC Book Manufacturers Ltd, Bridgend, Mid Glamorgan.

Contents

Preface   vii

Chapter 1 The Role of Research in Nursing   1

Chapter 2 Making a Start in Research   7

Chapter 3 Searching the Literature   16

Chapter 4 Evaluating Published Research   26

Chapter 5 Research Design   39

Chapter 6 Experimental Methods   54

Chapter 7 Surveys   70

Chapter 8 Qualitative Techniques   104

Chapter 9 Data Analysis   117

Chapter 10 Ethical Issues in Research   141

Chapter 11 Communicating Results   149

Chapter 12 Writing a Research Proposal   158

Chapter 13 Audit and Research   168

Chapter 14 The Future for Nursing Research   174

Epilogue   180

Glossary   181

Index   186

*To our families for
their patience
and our colleagues for
their support*

Preface

All too often the word 'Research' sends a *frisson* of fear through many nurses and health care professionals! The purpose of this book is to show that research is really quite a 'friendly', everyday activity. It is hard work sometimes, but satisfying and straightforward if you follow a systematic, problem-solving approach.

Why is it important for nurses to know about research? The Briggs report (Committee on Nursing, 1972, Cmnd 5115, HMSO) urged nurses to keep up to date with research, and policy statements from professional organisations and the DoH alike have emphasised nursing as a research-based profession. Nurse training is now academically based, thus challenging nursing to confirm and develop its body of knowledge. Far-reaching changes to the NHS have required nurses to rethink the way they practise and demonstrate that the care they give is not based on habit or trial and error, but is well thought out and based on sound evidence of effectiveness. With the current emphasis upon quality assurance and accountability, it is also important for nurses to be able to evaluate and justify their practice.

This new edition takes account of these changes with chapters on the role of nursing research in the new NHS, audit and its relationship to research and the introduction of a national strategy for funding and developing research which will contribute to health care services.

The book has two aims: first, to help close the gap between what is known and what is done in nursing practice by giving enough familiarity with the research process to understand and evaluate relevant research findings; and secondly to develop skills so that individuals can design and implement small-scale research projects which examine their own work critically. The book therefore operates at two levels, research appreciation and beginning actual research.

This is essentially a self-instruction guide to research methods. Practical exercises and activities are suggested in each chapter to promote the relevant skills for a research project. A range of quantitative and qualitative methods are discussed as options to solving research problems.

Each chapter works through the research process from the origins of the idea, through the research design, to the analysis and communication of results. We have also used a fictitious nursing research project at various points throughout the book, to illustrate the pleasures and the pains of research. The decisions made by a team of nurses in hospital and in the community in investigating the implications of a proposed change in policy are used to demonstrate the various techniques and issues.

With the growth of degree courses for nurses there is now a plethora of textbooks on research methodology, many from the United States, to cater for the growing interest and needs in nursing. Many are based on a step-by-step approach or describe exemplars in nursing research. This book is designed as a complete introductory workbook, however, aimed at nurses who have little or no knowledge of 'research', combined with the use of a running exemplar to give the essential details of research in a lively, relevant way. This second edition remains essentially the same as the first, while recognising and incorporating the changing context in which it will be read and, hopefully, utilised.

The book therefore has a wide appeal. Individual nurses and midwives of all grades and specialties could use it for updating and professional development as recommended by current policies. The workbook approach could be helpful to tutors teaching groups from basic to post-basic levels of education, where 'research awareness' is now part of the curriculum, and may involve some project work. The exercises in each chapter can be adapted for both individual and group work. The book could serve as a foundation for more formal research training such as the ENB 870 course, degree and diploma courses and research degrees. Although aimed mainly at nurses, it may also be of interest to allied caring professionals such as paramedics, therapists, health educators and social workers, who are similarly interested in research.

Both of the authors have considerable experience in conducting research and teaching research methods on a wide range of nursing and community courses, from short courses to degree level. Wendy Couchman is Professor and Head of School of Education and Health Studies at South Bank University, London. Dr Jane Dawson is Clinical Audit Facilitator, Portsmouth Hospitals Trust. Jane Dawson's experience and research background have been in hospital and community services and her areas of research interest are clinical audit, quality assurance in general nursing and midwifery and professional accountability. Wendy Couchman has a professional and research background in services for people with learning disabilities. Her particular research interest is interaction between professionals and services users in health and social care settings.

WENDY COUCHMAN
JANE DAWSON
1995

1

The Role of Research in Nursing

Nursing, in both the way it is practised and the way it is taught, has changed enormously during the last ten years or so. The advance of medical technology in all areas of patient care has meant that nurses have had to learn skills that are highly technical and increasingly specialised. Changes in the way health care is organised and the expectations society, patients and their relatives and friends have concerning care present nurses daily with new challenges and increasing demands.

It is no coincidence that the training of nurses has also changed, with more and more nursing courses, basic and advanced, being located in institutions of Higher Education and being taught at degree and higher degree level. This is a welcome move, but it is not without its problems. One of these is that within such settings nurses are being challenged to define the scientific basis of nursing practice and to demonstrate that a unique body of knowledge which has academic credibility exists; indeed, is being constantly refined and advanced.

This increasing emphasis on research is consistent with the transition of nursing away from being an occupation to becoming a profession. Sociologists have shown (Schröck, 1987) that such changes in status are characterised by elements such as:

1. The length of training being increased.
2. Assessment and examinations becoming more rigorous as the means of qualification.
3. More focus on research to establish a unique body of knowledge or theory.

Kim (1984) suggests that there are three aspects from which nurses use knowledge about research: first, utilising the underlying research skills and qualities in problem solving, second, employing the process and methods needed to conduct formal research and third – and perhaps most important – using research findings as 'research consumers'. Most nursing courses these days contain a research module, yet many nurses fail to base their practice on research-based knowledge.

Hunt (1984) listed four main reasons why nurses do not use research findings:

1. *Lack of knowledge*: Nurses are not aware of relevant research, have poor access to libraries or do not know how to evaluate and apply the findings.
2. *Disbelief*: Nurses do not believe research that challenges traditional practice.
3. *Lack of permission*: Nurses may not be allowed to challenge traditional practice by introducing change suggested by research.
4. *Lack of incentive*: Nurses are not rewarded for introducing change by positive feedback or by financial or status incentives.

With the advent of primary nursing and the concept of the 'named nurse' some of these barriers are, or should be, changing. Ensuring that nursing became a research-based profession was one of the core targets in the DoH Strategy for Nursing (Department of Health, 1990), and this means not simply *doing* research but *using* it. There is now a wealth of knowledge from nursing research started by the classic RCN studies of the 1960s and 1970s. However, the gap which still exists between what is known and what is done is graphically documented by Walsh and Ford (1989). They examined a number of everyday nursing situations, citing the research evidence for and against the practices which nurses commonly employ. Walsh and Ford came to the conclusion that nursing is all too frequently based on ward folk ritual and mythology. Many practices persist because 'they have always been done this way.'

Nurses also need to provide data to justify their practice in the increasingly political and economic arena of health care. Evidence will be required that services are effective. Practitioners must enter into a dialogue on what is to be measured and how, rather than leaving it to others who may not take some important factors into account. The process of providing that evidence through examining the quality and outcomes of clinical care is known as clinical audit. Research has an important part to play in audit and nurses who understand and can utilise research will be much better equipped to conduct valid audit projects. This subject is dealt with in more detail later in the book.

Another factor is that in 1991 the Department of Health published a Research and Development Strategy (Department of Health, 1991) and increased very significantly the funding for research in the NHS. A Taskforce was established in 1992 by the Chief Nursing Officer to consider the implications and opportunities of the Strategy for nurses. As a consequence nurses in all areas of clinical practice are increasingly likely to become aware of research activities. Knowing a little about research will help nurses understand what is going on when they, their clinical area, or patients and clients they care for become involved. The book will discuss the DoH (1991) Strategy for Research and the DoH (1993) Taskforce Report later in Chapter 14 on education and funding for research.

WHAT IS RESEARCH?

If research is defined as:

'An attempt to extend knowledge through systematic, scientific enquiry' (Hockey, 1986)

then most nurses possess the necessary skills to carry out and use research. The nursing process requires similar systematic procedures be applied to individual patients. Scientific enquiry is really a problem-solving model: the application of some basic skills in a series of logical steps:

1. A problem is stated.
2. An hypothesis is formulated for testing (i.e. a possible explanation is suggested).
3. Facts are gathered from observation or experimentation.
4. These facts are interpreted to see if the hypothesis was right.
5. Conclusions are drawn about possible solutions to the problem.

For centuries the scientific approach has been regarded as the finest way to establish new knowledge. Certainly, in nursing research it is considered to be more reliable as a means of finding out facts than the alternatives offered by tradition, authority or trial and error. This applies not only to the development of new knowledge, but also to checking existing knowledge through replication studies. Nursing needs to base clinical practice on sound evidence if it is to develop as a discipline. The principles of scientific research and the debate between different methods and degrees of scientific rigour will be discussed more fully in Chapter 5 on research design.

STRUCTURE OF THE BOOK

This book has been structured around the steps in the research process which are followed whether you are doing a research project or reading about one. It is laid out sequentially so that, like Alice, you can start at the beginning and go on until you reach the end. Alternatively, if you are only interested in one topic at a time, each chapter does make sense when read separately. At various points throughout the book are a number of Scenarios, each demonstrating how a particular topic might be tackled in a 'real life' situation. There are also exercises which you might like to try, either as you read through the book, or when you have finished to test just how much you have learnt!

You will see that the series of steps in research follows the same logical process as the scientific approach outlined earlier:

1. Stating research problem or question.
2. Reviewing relevant literature.
3. Choosing research design.
4. Collecting data.
5. Analysing data.
6. Discussing results.
7. Reporting results.

The process is in fact more *cyclic* (Figure 1.1) because there may be several points in a study where the researcher either refers back to an

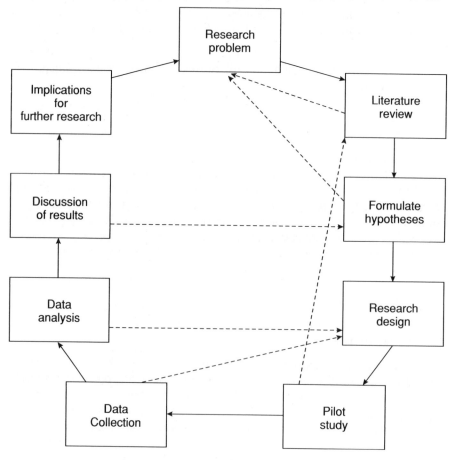

Figure 1.1 The research cycle

earlier step or repeats certain steps to refine the design. A completed study also raises questions to be pursued in other research.

GUIDE TO READING

The early stages of choosing and reading around a research topic and step-by-step techniques for reading research critically are covered in Chapters 3 and 4. Chapter 5 addresses the issues at the research design stage. Chapters 6 to 8 present a range of different styles, while Chapter 9 is on the analysis of data and its presentation. Associated matters such as ethics are dealt with in Chapter 10. The final steps in the research process are discussed in the last few chapters of the book. Chapter 11 deals with different media for the communication and publication of research findings, while how to write a research proposal is covered in Chapter 12. The relationship between clinical audit and research is covered in Chapter 13, and the future for nursing research, including funding, is discussed in Chapter 14.

Note

The feminine pronoun 'she' will be used throughout in the generic sense to mean 'he' or 'she'. Similarly, 'nurse' is used to denote all branches of nursing, midwifery and health visiting.

REFERENCES

Department of Health (1991) *Research for Health: A Research and Development Strategy for the NHS*. London: HMSO.

Department of Health (1993) *Report of the Taskforce on the Strategy for Research in Nursing, Midwifery and Health Visiting*. London: HMSO.

Department of Health Nursing Division (1990) *A Strategy for Nursing: A Report of the Steering Committee*. (Chairman Anne Poole). London: HMSO.

Hockey L (1986) *Nursing Research: Mistakes and Misconceptions*. Edinburgh: Churchill Livingstone.

Hunt J (1984) Why don't we use these findings? *Nursing Mirror*, **158** (8): 29.

Kim H S (1984) Critical contents of research process for an undergraduate nursing curriculum. *Journal of Nursing Education*, **23** (2): 70–72.

Schröck R A (1987) Professionalisation – a critical examination. *Recent Advances in Nursing*, **18**: 12–24.

Walsh M and Ford P (1989) *Nursing Rituals: Research and Rational Action*. Oxford: Butterworth-Heinemann.

FURTHER READING

Briggs A (Chairman) (1972) *Report of the Committee on Nursing*. Cmnd. 5115. London: HMSO.

Class S J and Cheater F M (1994) Utilization of nursing research: culture, interest and support. *Journal of Advanced Nursing*, **19**(4): 762–773.

McFarlane J (1970) *The Proper Study of the Nurse*. London: Royal College of Nursing.

McFarlane J (1980) Nursing as a research-based profession. *Nursing Times*, **76**(13).

Moores J (1987) The nurse v. leg ulcers. *Journal of District Nursing*, **5**(9): 16–21.

Powers B A and Knapp T R (1990) *A Dictionary of Nursing Theory and Research*. London: Sage Publications.

Treece E W and Treece J W (1977) *Elements of Research in Nursing*. New York: Mosby.

Walsh M and Ford P (1989) *Nursing Rituals: Research and Rational Action*. Oxford: Butterworth-Heinemann.

2

Making a Start in Research

True research is not simply a matter of gathering information. It is finding answers to questions or solutions to problems. Everyday practice can give rise to problems which niggle or puzzle and some of the best nursing research has been inspired by such problems. Practitioners can therefore sometimes make the best researchers, rather than someone from outside, as practitioners are in the best position to judge what are the important factors. We would also argue that the practitioner is in an ideal position for communicating and implementing ideas from the research. A systematic research attitude will in turn inform practice. The ability to be objective is of course vital.

Simply stated, both the researcher and the nurse need to question practice continually and challenge taken-for-granted assumptions in the same way that they did on their first day in the job. Ideas for research projects can also be generated through reading and study, as we will see later.

Unfortunately, finding research ideas is a difficult and uncomfortable process, accompanied by feelings of vagueness, aimlessness and indecision. It can be reassuring to recognise that this is a necessary state in the evolution of any creative activity. Even Einstein must have gone through the agonising process to reach his brilliant 'hunches'!

Although it is a creative process there are ways of introducing structure to minimise the pain and maximise opportunities for ideas, which we will show through some exercises. Most of these are based on the problem-solving model:

1. Define the problem.
2. Generate possible solutions.
3. Select and implement the best solution.
4. Evaluate the outcome.

Thinkers such as Edward de Bono (1970) promote the positive value of spending time at this stage to explore a problem fully, through lateral thinking and brainstorming. It is therefore wise to relax and not rush in order to make the right choices, or choices that you won't regret later. Practise your brainstorming skills with this exercise.

Exercise

Imagine that you have been cast ashore on a desert island naked, with nothing but a belt! What could you do with the belt?

Rules
1. Think of as many ideas as possible – spend at least 5 minutes on this stage.
2. Aim for quantity not quality at this stage – keep an open mind.
3. Do not spend too long on each idea – keep them bubbling.
4. Do not criticise or dismiss any suggestions yet.
5. Write everything down, however nonsensical or outrageous it seems – apparently silly or irrelevant ideas can often lead to a new way of looking at a problem.

When the ideas begin to dry up look again at your list. Now you can be critical and evaluate. Which seems the most feasible? Can you combine elements of several ideas?

Can you see that you are likely to have come up with a better solution than if you had taken the first idea that occurred to you, which is the usual 'vertical' thinking or logic?

Discussion
Obviously there are no right answers with this approach. People who do the exercise become very imaginative with possibilities of using the belt in different ways – ranging from using it as a source of food, as various tools, utensils and weapons, even as a means of ending it all! They usually end up with an optimum combination of uses. Now try brainstorming a list of researchable ideas in your field of nursing.

Exercise

Where do research problems come from?
Use the headings below as prompts to jot down ideas and questions. These three areas are the main sources for research topics in nursing.

Experience (the most common source of ideas)
Things that are puzzling, problematic or challenging in everyday practice, such as instructions on use of medication on discharge from hospital, effective communication between professionals.

Questions to ask:

- Why do we do this ...?
- Why this way ...?
- Who is it for ...?
- What if ...?

Reading
Ideas that arise from relevant literature; gaps left in research; need for replication; recommendations for research from other studies; contributions to a current issue or debate in the professional journals (e.g. the nursing process, treatment of pressure sores).
Questions to ask:

- Would that work here ...?
- What next ...?

Theory
Translating and testing theoretical concepts in the real world (e.g. nursing models, communication theories); adding to the body of nursing knowledge.
Questions to ask:

- What does that mean in practice ...?
- Can that be proved ...?

Discussion
In practice you would spend some time exploring ideas, sounding out colleagues, family and friends – providing they are prepared to follow the rules of brainstorming and suspend all criticism at this stage!

Ideally you would find a mentor with whom to discuss your ideas and the project as it progressed. This could be a colleague, a manager or a tutor. Gradually you would begin sorting and prioritising your list of potential research projects to narrow the focus and to select the most feasible idea.

CHOOSING A TOPIC

Here is a checklist of questions to help you choose more critically the most feasible topic from your list.

Exercise

Ask these questions about each of the possible topics on your list to decide which is the most researchable. You may find it helpful to work through the questions and the list with other people.

Is it really a problem?

- Is it only me who sees it as a problem?
- Who else finds it is a problem?

Is it a significant problem?

- Is it important?
- Is it too trivial?
- Will it benefit anyone?
- Will it be useful?
- Will it increase knowledge?
- Will it check assumptions?
- Will it inform policy or practice?

Is it a researchable problem?

- Is it morally, ethically or politically dubious?
- Do I need permission from the Ethical Committee?
- Is it too philosophical?
- Can it be precisely defined and measured?
- Do I have the necessary knowledge and skills?

How feasible is it?

- Is there time?
- Are people available?
- Will they consent and co-operate?
- What facilities and equipment are needed?
- How much will it cost?
- Do I have financial support?
- Is it worth it?
- Is it familiar?

Is it interesting?

- Is it newsworthy?
- Will anyone care?
- Do I care enough?

Discussion

All of these questions represent important considerations, not least the last. It is vital that one is made curious and excited by the topic from the outset in order to be sustained through the 'dark days' when things go wrong, or in the middle of a project when you seem a long way from the beginning and a long way from the end. You need to 'own' the project.

Beware of being persuaded to follow someone else's idea or hobbyhorse – it will be difficult to stay motivated.

RESEARCH STATEMENTS

A check-list helps the beginner researcher to reach a decision on the broad topic. The next stage is to refine the topic to a written, formal statement of the problem or question to be answered by the research design. This clarifies thinking and involves some detailed planning of specific areas of interest. If you can get this right at the start, the project will be much easier to follow and achieve.

For example, the topic 'nurse–patient interaction' is too broad and likely to lead the researcher up many interesting avenues which go nowhere in particular. The topic is open to too many interpretations, all potentially researchable if the terms are defined more precisely, as follows.

Broad topic

- Nurse–patient interaction

Researchable topics

- The importance of touch in communication with elderly people.
- Asking questions of women in labour.
- The teaching of counselling skills to student nurses.
- Giving information to children before an operation.
- Social skills training with psychiatric patients.
- Instructions to heart patients leaving hospital.
- Telephone links with 'at risk' patients in the community.

Writing research statements is, of course, similar to writing objectives in the nursing process and the same general principles apply: the communication of clear, unambiguous statements of intent. In other words, you avoid 'fuzzies'!

Exercise

Which of the following research statements are fuzzies?

1. Looking at hospital visitors.
2. The effects of reorganisation on the ward sister's role.
3. Interaction between professionals in the psychiatric team.
4. Use of the nursing process.
5. District Nurses' rating of stress factors in their work load.
6. Confidentiality of patient records.

Discussion
Statements 1, 4 and 6 are fuzzy, 2, 3 and 5 are non-fuzzy.

The test for a fuzzy is whether or not it is difficult to know exactly what the researcher intends, or if the statement is open to misinterpretation. As a further exercise you could try restating the fuzzies in non-fuzzy terms, relevant to your own field.

Fuzzy words are vague abstractions ('being words'), whereas non-fuzzy words suggest performance ('doing words').

Fuzzies	*Non-fuzzies*
knowing	comparing
understanding	contrasting
appreciating	constructing
believing	identifying
developing	defining
internalising	discriminating
enjoying	sorting

Sometimes it is difficult to express intentions fully in non-fuzzy performance terms and in these cases you need to describe how you are going to indicate or measure the abstract quality. If, for example, you were interested in attitudes about a particular subject, you would need to consider the means of assessing these, whether by interview or rating scale or some other method.

The refinement of a research statement is a continuing process until a formal written statement of the problem is reached. This should cover 'who does what, when and how'. The statement must also specify outcome and not just the process of the research – the 'ends' as well as the 'means'. To summarise, a research statement should spell out detail explicitly, so that anyone could read it and have a good idea of what the researcher was intending to do.

Figure 2.1 is an illustration of how our example of nurse–patient interaction could be translated into a workable research statement by successive steps.

It is sometimes easier to restate the topic as a question, as this seems to give a sense of urgency or drive to find the answers by the research process. Sometimes you might want to develop the research statement further to an hypothesis, but this would normally be after the literature search stage. We will discuss hypothesis in a later chapter. Remember also that you are not concerned with how to answer the research question (i.e. the method) at this stage, otherwise the methodological tail tends to wag the dog. Do not assume yet, for instance, that you need to do a survey simply because a great deal of research tends to use that method. There may be other methods more appropriate as a means of answering your question.

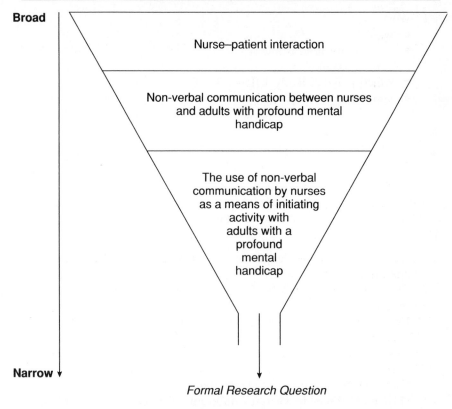

Broad

Nurse–patient interaction

Non-verbal communication between nurses
and adults with profound mental
handicap

The use of non-verbal
communication by nurses
as a means of initiating
activity with
adults with a
profound
mental
handicap

Narrow

Formal Research Question

Can non-verbal communication be used effectively by
nurses as a means of initiating leisure activities
with adults with a profound mental handicap in a
residential setting?

Figure 2.1 Translating a research problem into a research question

SCENARIO

Getting started

Ward 4 is to become a day-surgery and 5-day unit in the near future.
The staff have many questions as to how this will affect them and their
practice. The ward team decide the best way to answer some of these is
to use research, both that conducted by others and published in the journals, and also to carry out some small studies themselves. After discussing
the new policy and the problems it might bring with colleagues and other
professionals the team, together with the local Community Nurse, decide
to have a brainstorming session, listing thoughts as they occur on a sheet
of paper. This is what the list looked like:

1. Work-load
   - ward
   - community (extra time?)
2. Present situation
   - which patients likely 1 day/5 days?
   - which longer stays?
   - how change nursing process – different models – how work for surgery?
   - records – old or new needed?
   - patients' views, feelings – new and traditional systems?

From this list the team defined a series of questions leading to a number of possible projects, with a different yet complementary angle on the problem. The list of questions (checked for fuzzies!) finally looked like this:

1. What is the average length of stay at present for various types of operations on this ward?
2. Which operations will be 5-day stays, which will be a day, which longer than 5 days?
3. How have similar wards adapted the nursing process to the new policy?
4. How would a different model of the nursing process work on our ward?
5. How will the proposed changes affect patients on the ward?
6. How much time do visits to different types of patients take after discharge from hospital?
7. Will the new system mean longer visits to patients?
8. Will the present type of nursing documentation be suitable for the new system?

Exercise

Think of a problem or question from your own clinical area, then write down as quickly as possible all the words or aspects you can think of in connection with it. You could involve friends or colleagues in this. When you can't think of any more, try refining them into questions. Finally, check for fuzzies!

REFERENCE

de Bono E (1970) *Lateral Thinking: A Textbook of Creativity.* Harmondsworth: Penguin Books.

FURTHER READING

Abbott P and Sapsford R (eds) (1992) *Research into Practice: a Reader for Nurses and the Caring Professions*. Buckingham: Open University Press.

Ashworth P (1990) *Bridges of Opportunity: Research Linking Nursing Practice, Education and Management*. London: Royal College of Nursing.

Bell J (1994) *Doing Your Research Project*. Buckingham: Open University Press.

Calnan J (1984) *Coping with Research, the Complete Guide for Beginners*. London: Heinemann Medical Books.

Clifford C and Gough S (1990) *Nursing Research: a Skill-based introduction*. Hemel Hempstead: Prentice Hall.

Cormack D F S (ed.) (1991) *The Research Process in Nursing*, 2nd edn, ch. 6. Oxford: Blackwell.

Darling V H and Rogers J (1986) *Research for Practising Nurses*, ch. 2. Basingstoke: Macmillan.

Macleod Clark J and Hockey L (eds) (1989) *Further Research for Nursing: a New Guide for the Enquiring Nurse*. London: Scutari Press.

Polit D and Hungler B (1983) *Nursing Research: Principles and Methods*, ch. 5. Philadelphia: J B Lippincott.

Robinson K and Robinson H (1992) *What is Research?* London: Distance Learning Centre, South Bank Polytechnic.

Sheehan J (1985) Research Series 1: Starting the study. *Nursing Mirror*, **160**(18): 17–18.

Treece E W and Treece J W (1977) *The Elements of Research in Nursing*. New York: Mosby.

3

Searching the Literature

Probably the one factor which will have most influence on the way you go about your research is the literature search. If you read any major research report you will find that a large part of it is devoted to a review of the literature. Why is this? Why does it matter so much? When – and how – should it be done?

The first point to make is that the literature search is not something that is simply done once and then forgotten. It is almost a continuous process throughout a project, although concentrated and directed according to the stage reached in the research. The main literature search, which is carried out at the beginning of a research project, will probably take about one-third to one-half of the total time available to conduct the project. After that the literature is consulted for specific reasons: to help the development of the research tools, for example, or to look for explanatory theory after the data has been analysed.

PRELIMINARY SEARCH

When you start to think about a certain subject and how research might be carried out into this, a review of the literature is essential. The aim at this stage is to gain an overview of the subject, to 'read around' it. This stage is very general, but inevitably it will become more focused as you begin to identify more clearly what it is you wish to do.

DIRECTED LITERATURE SEARCH

As the thinking about the subject becomes more focused, so the literature search becomes more directed and specific regarding certain points, as follows:

1. *The research question.* From a vague idea of a subject you wish to know more about, the literature can help to define the precise

research question it is intended to answer. It will also help in formulating an hypothesis if the research is of a design which requires this.

2. *The research design.* The decisions that have to be made on the most appropriate way of going about answering that research question will be aided by reading about previous studies. Seeing how other people tackled the same or similar research question will demonstrate the advantages and pitfalls in various types of research design.

3. *The research tools.* You may find during a literature search that someone has used a particular questionnaire or other measurement technique that you feel it would be appropriate to use, or adapt. As long as you can justify the application of that tool in the study, there is no reason why you should not do so.

4. *The research criteria.* Reading how other researchers have defined the variables in previous studies will provide some ideas about the definitions you will use. A variable is a unit (person, event or characteristic) which can vary. Age is a variable, nursing qualifications and attendance at outpatients are all variables. If, for example, the research concerns non-attenders at outpatients clinics, precisely what is meant by non-attenders? Anyone who misses just one appointment, or people who attend some appointments but miss some? The literature search will help you decide where best to direct your efforts.

5. *Theory.* The thorny question of how and where theory fits into research can only be resolved by reference to the literature. Reading the work of others may bring to your attention theory relevant to the research topic which you decide to test out, or apply in a different way. Equally, you may come across theoretical ideas with which you disagree, but at least this will serve to sharpen up your own thinking. If you started out without a clear theoretical framework before the data was collected, then the literature may give meaning and explanation to the findings through theory generated by previous work.

Another way to think about the literature search is (a) research which has been done by others on the same subject, and (b) research which is related in some way but was carried out in other areas. For example, if you were interested in the cause and effect of stress in nurses it would be useful to look at published material on stress in teachers or some other occupational groups.

PURPOSES OF THE LITERATURE SEARCH

The purpose of the literature search, then, is to:

1. Find out what other research has already been conducted on the topic, or a related topic.

2. Give ideas on the research design and methodology, and tools which could be appropriately applied.
3. Aid in the definition of the variables in the intended research.
4. Consider the theoretical framework which will underpin the study.
5. Put the project into the context of the broader body of knowledge in the field.

The literature reviewed can be of two kinds, research and non-research. Research literature, as it implies, reports on specific projects or studies conducted according to research principles. Non-research literature covers the opinions, experiences and theories which have some bearing on the subject, or which relate to it in some way.

HOW TO CARRY OUT A LITERATURE SEARCH

Hospitals and schools of nursing usually have very good libraries, and this is the place to start. Many hospitals now have postgraduate centres on site which all staff can consult and this will enlarge the range of material available. The one nearest to you will probably be linked to others in the health region and to the British Library. This means that the library will be able to borrow books and obtain photocopies of articles which appeared in journals it does not itself hold. There may be a charge for this service, however, so find out about this. Your library will also have a catalogue of the journals it does take, which may show the journal holdings of other libraries in your region.

If there is a university, polytechnic, or college of further education within reach, then the range of literature available to you opens up enormously. Most such establishments have some form of link with the health district, so it is worth contacting the librarian to find out what arrangements there are for health authority employees to borrow from them.

The local authority library is well worth investigating, and there are also specialist libraries which concentrate on particular fields of study. A list of some of these is given at the end of this chapter. Whichever library you are using, don't be afraid to ask advice from the librarian. Librarians are specially trained to assist people in carrying out searches or helping to locate particular material. They will not do the work for you, however; it is still your responsibility, but you will save yourself a great deal of time and trouble by seeking their help.

The first thing to do when embarking on a literature search is to write down a list of 'key words'. This means words which are central to the research topic. The best way to do this is to state the research problem as simply as possible, trying to reduce it to one or two sentences. If you look back at Chapter 2 on refining the research statement, the importance of this stage and the technique of how to do this are discussed more fully.

Once you have your formal written statement, then pick out the words which are central to this statement.

Another way into the literature is to list the authors whom you happen to know have written on the subject, then look up their work.

When you start your search there are four main sources of information.

BIBLIOGRAPHIES

Bibliographies are lists of published material such as books, articles and sometimes papers given at conferences. These are listed both by subject (where your keywords become useful) and by author. The author, title, place and date of publication are given.

ABSTRACTS

These are similar to bibliographies, but in addition a summary of the material is also given. The abstract may simply outline the subject of the paper, without the results, or it may include the main results. This is particularly useful, as then you can decide whether a particular publication is relevant to your needs before searching it out or sending for it.

INDEXES

Again, material is listed both by subject and by author but only articles are given, not books. Most indexes scan journals internationally for material to be included, so not all the references you find will be available in English, or they may be in journals which are not collected by many libraries in this country.

Bibliographies are usually in the form of booklets. Indexes are much weightier in size and content! A list of Bibliographies, Abstracts and Indexes is given later in this chapter.

This information is also held on microfiche. These are small acetate sheets, each of which holds a large number of entries, and which are read under a special viewer. The fiches are usually classified alphabetically by author and title, with a separate alphabetical set of subject fiches. Virtually every library has microfiche these days, so they are worth investigating.

The main drawback with abstracts and indexes is that they take time to compile, so it may be several months after the date of publication before a paper is included in them. Indeed, because the cycle of research, presentation and publication as thesis, article and book, is such a painstaking and time-consuming affair, there can be an interval of 4 or 5 years between commencing the research and its final appearance in an abstract or index. Current awareness facilities, such as the Health Information Service, can help to fill the gap. There are also registers that list the current research in colleges and universities. The librarian will be able to help in identifying these. Some libraries run their own current awareness service.

Before you start searching the bibliographies, abstracts or indexes, one essential step is to consult the list of subject headings covered. This will be found in a separate booklet, and is important because the subject you are searching for may appear under a slightly different classification than your 'keyword'.

Another source which may prove useful is encyclopaedias. Apart from *Encyclopaedia Britannica*, there are encyclopaedias dealing with particular fields of learning such as medicine or nursing. Again, use the skills of the librarian to help track down these and other sources of information.

COMPUTER SEARCHING AND CD-ROM

During the 1960s many libraries became equipped to conduct literature searches by computer, linking up via a telephone link with a main data base which could be situated anywhere in the world. The one of most use in the field of health is called Medline. Obviously this is a much more complex undertaking, and needs a librarian to authorise and institute the link. It is also very expensive. However, computer searches have now been largely overtaken by what is known as CD-ROM, which stands for Compact Disc Read Only Memory. The compact disc looks exactly the same as those used for playing music, but instead contains a database of published material gathered from hundreds of journals and other sources, which it displays on a computer screen. There are different CD-ROM products depending on the type of information the database contains. For instance, there are CD-ROM products on water resources, legal matters and human nutrition. In the field of health, Medline and a nursing data-base CINAHL (Cumulative Index of Nursing and Allied Health) are probably most relevant. CD-ROM has revolutionised literature searching, as once you have been shown what to do it is very easy to scan an enormous number of published articles quite quickly.

The time-lag between publication of an article and its inclusion in the database has also been shortened considerably, as new up-to-date discs are produced regularly. CD-ROM provides a number of options. You can scan a list of articles, choose the ones where you wish to read the abstracts, then print out the abstracts you decide are of most use. Finally, you can go to the journal in which the article appeared, or arrange to obtain a photocopy of the article.

Once you have obtained one or two articles or books you will find that these contain references which you can then follow up. This is known as the 'snowball' method. In fact, this can become rather dangerous and turn into more of an avalanche! It is very tempting to follow every lead in the hope that it will prove useful, or because it looks interesting. Resist! Otherwise you will end up with masses of material, much of it irrelevant. Think what you are looking for, and ask yourself how the reference will contribute to the research. Once you have found a suitable reference then the next step is to read the original article, if the journal is taken by your library, or ask the librarian to obtain a photocopy from a library where it is held. If the reference relates to a book then that too should be obtained. It is not sufficient simply to note that certain work has been published on the subject in question; you must read the original material. When you find yourself coming across references that have already been noted, then you have probably gone far enough in that area and should move on.

Certain subjects may turn out to have been extensively researched already, with a considerable amount of existing literature. This does not necessarily mean that the research you plan must be abandoned, but it does mean that it will require careful thought and planning. There are two ways of coping with this situation. First, it is perfectly valid to replicate previous research. This means that the original project is repeated as closely as possible, to see if the results are repeated. Clearly, the implication of this is that the tools used, the type of sample and all other variables must match the original research. Replication is very valuable but unfortunately does not have the glamour of original research, so is too little exercised in nursing research. The second approach is to supply a different angle to the original work: repeating a research tool on a different sample, for instance, or a different tool on the same type of sample, or testing a new theory on the same research topic. As long as you can support your new approach through logical argument and use of the literature then there is no reason why the project should not go ahead.

Points to remember

1. Literature searching is often slow to begin with, so do not get discouraged.
2. You will need to go to more indexes if you find that there are not many references for your subject.
3. Most indexes have an author list as well as a subject list. If you know the author of an article or book on your topic, look to see if they have other published work.
4. Journals have their own cumulative index, usually compiled annually. This is useful if you know of a journal catering for a specialist need, e.g. *Intensive Care Nursing*.
5. Use the reference lists at the end of books and articles.

KEEPING TRACK

Whenever you visit the library during your search be sure to take a note-book and pencil with you, so that you can note down references you wish to follow up. Make sure you have enough information to find the reference when you need it again.

One absolutely essential thing to do is to have some system of recording the references you read. One simple method is to use postcards or similar as a Kardex. On one side write the title, author, date and source of publication. If this is a journal then the full journal title, the date published, the title of the article, the volume, number and page numbers must all be recorded. For books, you should record the author, title, publishing company and date and place of publication, for example:

Watson J (1981) Nursing's scientific quest.
Nursing Outlook, July, **29**(7): 413–416.
Abrams M (1977) Beyond Three Score Years and Ten.
Mitchum: Age Concern.

On the back of the card write a brief summary of the contents, so that you can refer quickly to relevant material at a later date. Just how you catalogue is a matter of personal preference. It could be alphabetically by author, grouped by subject. You could even duplicate your references and have one alphabetical and one by subject, then cross-reference them. If you have a computer then references can be kept on this, but make a note of exactly what each file on your reference disk contains or you will have to search them all each time you wish to refer to one.

LIBRARIES

The Royal College of Nursing Library
Extensive collection of nursing and related literature. Steinberg Collection of Theses. Information service available. Open to nurses, postal lending service to members.

The Librarian, Royal College of Nursing, 20 Cavendish Square, London W1M 0AB. Tel. 0171–409 3333.

The King's Fund Library
Literature on a wide range of health care issues. Service open to genuine enquiries.

The Librarian, King's Fund Centre, 126 Albert Street, London NW1 7NF. Tel. 0171–267 6111.

The Department of Health and Social Security
Several different libraries. Access by appointment only on written application to librarian. Starting point option:

Library and Information Systems Directorate, Skipton House, 80 London Road, London SE1 6LW. Tel. 0171–972 2000

The Scottish Health Service Management Development Group
Literature on management, planning and administration of health services and related subjects. Open to all Scottish Health Service employees.

Crewe Rd South, Edinburgh EH4 2LF. Tel. 0131–332 2335

BIBLIOGRAPHIES, ABSTRACTS AND INDEXES

Royal College of Nursing Bibliography
Originally published monthly, now more sporadic.

Department of Health Nursing Research Abstracts
Published quarterly.

Department of Health Health Service Abstracts
Published monthly.

American Journal of Nursing Company International Nursing Index
Published monthly.

Index Medicus
Published quarterly. English and foreign language material listed on medical subjects.

SCENARIO

Literature searching

The ward team on Ward 4, a traditional surgical ward, have just learnt that the ward is to become day- and 5-day in the near future. While they are worried by the impending change the Ward Manager, Sister Hudson, suggests they should conduct a literature search to find out more about how 5-day wards work and how best to adapt their nursing practice to meet the new situation.

So now let's see how the ward team would tackle the literature search. It is important for them to work out who is going to do what, or they could end up all covering the same ground rather than extending and deepening the search. The team agree to keep a central index of references as well as their personal ones, so that they can each look through the references being generated to see which are relevant to them.

Sister Hudson's primary interest is the organisation and management of the ward in future. What kind of surgical procedures are likely to be done under the new policy? What are the implications for the way care is given and staff rotas arranged? She decides that she will look for reports and research studies on other one-day and five-day surgical schemes to see what kind of records or other data were collected there.

Sister Brown is a community nurse from the local health centre. On hearing of the change in Ward 4's admission policies her concern is how patients and their relatives will be affected and what kind of care will be needed by patients being discharged from the ward. How will it affect her work-load? Will she have more surgical dressings to do and if so, is she up to date in the newest techniques? In particular Sister Brown wants to know how best to liaise with the ward so as to pick out those patients who will require more care at home. The reports and studies Sister Hudson will be searching will obviously be her first point of contact, then from these she can pick out any references to community care needs. The next stage will depend very much on the findings from these as to what else to look for.

Student Nurse Green is interested in finding out what aspects are likely to worry patients most about going home after surgery, so she needs to search the literature for any work in which the patients' perspective was examined. There has been some work on this, but not all of it related to surgical patients. Nevertheless, Student Nurse Green will find that patients' attitudes to other types of health care may give her some ideas worth exploring. In addition, some of the basic psychology texts might prove useful in considering how people cope with frightening or stressful circumstances.

Staff Nurse Baker is interested in whether the change will provide a good opportunity to move to primary nursing. She will need to look first at some of the basic texts on the philosophy behind primary nursing and how its use has been evaluated. Her next task will be to find research on how nursing care has been given in other 5-day surgical wards, then finally to see if any of these have used a primary nursing model.

Our ward team might list the following key words from the series of questions that they defined.

Current length of stay (specific operations).
Day surgery and 5-day wards.
Use/evaluation of primary nursing.
Hospitals at home.
Patients' attitudes to surgery.
Coping with stress.

Can you think of any more? You might like to try the exercises given below, to see how much you remember from the chapter.

Exercises

1. Find a piece of research written during the last 3 years on your own specialty, using the indexes, bibliographies and abstracts mentioned.
2. Find a research paper, article or book on a particular topic, but applied to your own specialty, e.g. nurse–patient communication, again using the indexes, abstracts or bibliographies.

In a class situation the papers can be brought to the group, with an explanation of how the individual went about searching for it, where it was actually found, and any problems or false leads encountered.

FURTHER READING

Abdellah F and Levine C (1979) *Better Patient Care Through Nursing Research*, pp. 384–408. New York: Macmillan.
Macleod Clark J and Stodulski A (1978) How to find out: a guide to searching the literature. *Nursing Times*, **74**(6): 21–23.
Moorbath P (1988) A guide to nursing research literature. *Senior Nurse*, **8**(1): 35–36.
Pollock L (1984) 6 steps to a successful literature search. *Nursing Times*, **80**(44): 40–43.
Treece E W and Treece J W (1986) The library and computer-based literature searches. *Elements of Research in Nursing*, ch. 7, pp. 91–112. St Louis: Mosby.

4

Evaluating Published Research

Literature searching is time consuming, frustrating and requires much patience. It is also an exciting and enriching experience. However, if you are to gain from your search you need to learn how to read research critically. This is one of the most useful skills a nurse can acquire, whether or not she is engaged in research. Books and articles on research findings have much more meaning if read in this way, and the relevance and appropriateness of the findings to clinical practice can be more clearly evaluated.

Reading and making sense of research books and articles is a little like reading a detective story. The reader likes to be able to follow all the twists of the plot, trying to spot the clues for oneself, then deciding if on the evidence collected the author was justified in coming up with the solution that he/she presents. So it is with reading research – can you follow the threads of the argument, are some things missed and does the data support the research conclusions?

This seems a very daunting task to the beginner. How do you know what to look for? Can you not simply take it all on trust? After all, the work has been published, so it must be right, surely?

The answer is that there are almost certainly going to be elements of the work on which it is possible to hold different views. Besides, it is you the reader who needs to be convinced about the strength of the case. You want to know whether the research reported is valid and reliable. Only then will you be able to judge its relevance and application for you.

The main thing to bear in mind is that the author has (or should have) gone through the research process in carrying out the work reported on. By thinking about how the author went through the various stages there is a framework for the investigations. The key questions you need to ask are:

What was the study about?
Why was it done?

How was it done?
Are the findings explained, justified and relevant?

WHAT WAS THE STUDY ABOUT?

One of the difficulties in reviewing literature is that it is not always possible to decide what a work is all about by the title. How descriptive, then is the title of the work? An abstract or summary can help to show quickly whether or not it is relevant for your needs by giving an impression of the contents, so is there an abstract? Was the research worthwhile – is it a subject which is of concern and interest to nurses and nursing, or to other health-care disciplines?

WHY WAS THE STUDY DONE?

Does the piece explain why the writer chose to study that particular question? It could have been that it arose from his or her work, but does it say so? How the writer became involved in the subject in the first place can tell you how experienced he or she was, both in the field under study and also in conducting research. This latter point is important, as the research could have been conducted by someone very inexperienced in research techniques. This clearly will affect the quality of the work. Should this seem to be the case then is there any explanation of how the researcher was supervised – was there a supervisor or supervisory board? If the research was sponsored or funded by a particular body it could have had an influence on the research, so it is relevant to know how the research was funded. Just why was the research question formulated in the first place, and are the problem, research objectives and hypothesis clearly stated? Was there a Steering Committee who might have been influential in such decisions?

HOW WAS IT DONE?

First of all, what kind of research design was it: survey, interpretive or experimental? The design should always be appropriate to the research question, so ask yourself whether you feel this is so.

Another area to examine is the literature review. Look at the dates of the references – are they very old or up to date? If the topic is well known to you then you will be able to judge whether the review has included the most recent and important work or whether there are some serious omissions. How do the references and literature appear to have been used? Do they add to the arguments being presented or have they been 'tacked on' to give an appearance of scholarship to the work?

The author should also have defined clearly the terms used: how was 'non-compliance with diet' or other variables interpreted for the purpose of the research? Is that definition sensible?

If the research involved the use of a sample of any kind then the work should discuss how it was chosen, whether it was representative of the study population and whether it was adequate in size for the purpose.

The reasons for the rejection of possible alternative methods should be discussed, together with the pros and cons of the method which was used. Any research tools, such as questionnaires, should be explained as to their origin and testing and if a pilot study was conducted, whether changes were made subsequently. A full report should contain copies of measurement tools, usually as an appendix, but in an article one or two 'specimen' questions or part of the attitude scale gives some indication of the actual data collection method.

One of the areas sometimes unexplored in research publications is the ethical considerations of the study. It is worth thinking about ethical issues which you feel could have been involved. Does the author discuss these, and is there evidence of respondents being given the choice as to whether or not to participate?

ARE THE FINDINGS EXPLAINED, JUSTIFIED AND RELEVANT?

To begin with, the paper should contain an explanation of how the data was analysed. This applies to both qualitative and quantitative data. The use of computers in the analysis should be acknowledged, and information given as to the nature of statistical advice or supervision as appropriate.

When it comes to the results themselves the thing to ask yourself is can you as the reader understand them? Are tables and graphs clearly labelled, and can you work out what they are telling you? Do not be blinded by science – if you cannot make sense of the information presented then the author has failed in his/her basic task – communication and enlightenment.

Sometimes one or two statistical tests are given. Obviously you will not be able to interpret these without some statistical knowledge. Chapter 9 will examine quantitative data, and explain some of the statistical techniques used in its analysis. It is worth making yourself acquainted with the more frequent of such tests, then you can form your own impression as to the validity of the results. Even the use of percentages is worth examination. For example, if raw numbers are not also given the reader may not be made aware that the impressive figure of 90%, for instance, actually refers to nine people, where the total sample was 10.

Having examined the data do you feel that the author is justified in drawing the conclusions given? Go back to the stated hypothesis or research objectives to see how the results relate to these. There may well be gaps, omissions or assumptions, but if so these should be acknowledged and discussed. Look out for quantum leaps between the data and the conclusions drawn from them!

Finally, if the work included recommendations, either for research or for policy, do you consider that they are supported by the research? Do they flow from the findings, or appear to have been put in as an afterthought? Above all, are you convinced enough to implement them?

SUMMARY

The aim of reading research publications in this way is not to tear them to pieces and discard them, as there is always something to learn from any study. The aim is to make a reasoned judgement about the research. This takes skill and practice, but the questions to ask can be put into a check-list:

1. *Research problem* – is this stated in clear terms, and the reason for its generation explained?
2. *Influences, assumptions and limitations* – could the funding organisation, the nature of the research or the background and experience of the researcher have biased the results? Who gave advice or supervised the project?
3. *Literature and references* – how up to date and comprehensive is the researcher's knowledge of the subject? Is the literature well integrate into the arguments presented? Are theoretical concepts, if any, adequately discussed?
4. *Research objectives and hypothesis* – how well do these relate to the original research problem?
5. *Description of study* – is it clear whether the study is experimental, survey or interpretative? Are the nature of the population, the size of the sample and the definition of variables given?
6. *Research methodology* – why was that particular method chosen? How were research tools developed and are there examples of them? What was the response rate?
7. *Pilot study* – were changes made on the basis of the pilot study? If there was no pilot study, why was this?
8. *Ethical issues* – what ethical issues are relevant to the study, and how were these taken into account?
9. *Data analysis* – what form did this take? What statistical tests have been conducted? Can the reader understand the results fairly easily?
10. *Conclusions and recommendations* – how do these relate to the research aims? If all research aims have not been met, is this discussed? Has the hypothesis been proven? Could alternative hypotheses provide a better explanation of the results? Are the recommendations justified by the research as presented?

RESEARCH TERMINOLOGY

One of the stumbling blocks to reading research, or writing up your own, is that there are certain ways of expressing things which to the lay person sound like jargon. This is not surprising as research, like any other tradition of scholarship, has developed its own language, the purpose of which is not to mystify the reader but to enable practitioners to communicate more easily. Unfortunately, the existence of this research language means that it is all too easy for research publications to be written in a style that is unintelligible to many readers, creating an elitist perception of research, and a gap between the researcher and the nurse practitioner which does the cause of true nursing research no good at all. The best defence against this is to become familiar with research terminology and its usage. A glossary of research terms is given at the end of the book.

RESEARCH AWARENESS

Once you have learnt how to read research critically you will find that it alters your whole attitude to the nursing literature. The relevance and possible application to your speciality of the articles and books that you read becomes much more apparent and the findings and conclusions make far more sense. At this point you may find yourself beginning to collect copies of articles which interest you. The danger is that you will slowly sink under a mountain of paper unless you find a way of organising yourself and the material you read.

The easiest way to do this is to start a research awareness file. As the name implies, it is a file which is designed to keep you abreast of current developments in your field. One method of doing this is to get into the habit, at intervals of perhaps every 3 months or so, of looking through some of the bibliographies and indexes discussed earlier; or you could arrange with colleagues that each of you will scan a certain journal regularly, and then pool your findings (this is known as a Journal Club). Having listed the references which seem interesting, gradually read them in turn and with your newly acquired critical faculties pick out the ones you feel have most to offer. Then catalogue them as described, with a brief account of the contents on the back. You may decide to start a research awareness board on the ward, on which interesting references or photocopies of articles are pinned for everyone to see. You could either destroy the references to the articles you reject, or keep them separately in case you have a need for them at a later date. In practice it is probably safer to take the latter course as if you destroy references it is almost a certainty that you will need them one day!

Research critique

Staff Nurse Baker read an article on primary nursing which she had found in one of the journals and had thought it very interesting and useful. Then the tutor on her diploma course had mentioned the same article and had been quite critical of several points.

The team discussed this and realised that they all had the same problem. As beginners, how could they evaluate the standard and content of the research they were reading?

The ward team decide to try a critique of an article together, so that they will be in a better position when it comes to understanding the literature they are reading. The paper they choose is given below. You might like to try it yourself, before seeing what the ward team thought.

RESEARCH CRITIQUE EXEMPLAR

Where are they now? A survey of career patterns of
nursing diploma holders
Brenda Bedford MSc, BA, CSS, and the DPSN Year 2 Group

Background

In September 1986 a group of twelve second-year DPSN (Diploma in Professional Studies in Nursing) students and their tutor began a brainstorming session. It was intended to generate ideas for a group research project which formed part of the course curriculum. This exercise provoked thoughts on 'Why on earth are we doing this course anyway?' The natural progression of this train of thought led to speculation about previous students who had survived the rigours of the course and seen it through to completion. What had happened to them? Where were they now? After further discussion it was decided that this should form the subject of the research project.

The research was planned around two main assumptions:

1. That gaining a nursing diploma (DPSN or the London Diploma in Nursing) would stimulate nurses to make changes in their professional lives, either by moving away from the bedside and into nurse education, management or research or by taking further studies.
2. That there would be more changes in the career patterns of men than of women.

The other major problem facing them was that if a camel was a horse designed by a committee, what would a research project undertaken by

12 individuals turn out? With some trepidation the work was divided up and the literature search begun.

The review of the literature, like all other tasks in the project, was shared within the group. As well as nursing indexes and bibliographies an on-line computer search was conducted to find additional references.

Several recent studies had traced the career paths of students from post-basic nursing courses. Rogers[1] found that a high proportion of JBCNS certificate holders wished to stay in a clinical post. Montague and Herbert[2] and Kemp[3] showed a tendency for nursing degree graduates to stay in clinical nursing for the first few years. A commitment to continuing higher education and research activity was also shown by the graduates, and in studies of nursing education and nursing administration students by Hardy et al.[4] and Sinclair et al.[5]. Hardy noted that male students outnumbered female students on the nursing education certificate course.

Method

With the assumptions of the project and the literature in mind the group drafted a questionnaire which was 'piloted' on diploma holders locally and checked with statistical staff at the Dorset Institute. The final draft of the questionnaire included closed and open questions so that questions could be analysed both quantitatively and qualitatively

A sample of 20 diploma courses was selected by stratified random sampling to cover proportional numbers of DPNS and London Diploma courses at colleges and schools of nursing throughout the United Kingdom. To preserve confidentiality each course was sent 10 questionnaires with envelopes and asked to distribute them to a range of diploma students from the last 10 years (a total of 200 questionnaires). The response to the survey was more than 65%, even though no follow-up letter was possible.

Returned questionnaires were coded by the group, and they also partic-ipated in the data analysis by SPSS (a statistical package) at computer terminals, guided by the computer staff at the Dorset Institute.

Results

The results will be discussed with reference to the two main assumptions:

Assumption 1

It had been assumed that gaining the diploma would stimulate nurses to make changes in their professional lives, either by moving away from the bedside and into education, management or research, or by undertaking further studies. Of all respondents, 65% had had a change in career since the diploma and 46% felt this change had been influenced by the course.

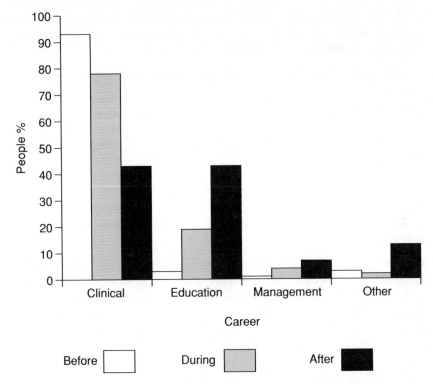

Figure 4.1 Careers before, during and after the diploma

Figure 4.1 shows career patterns of diploma holders before, during and after gaining the diploma. There is a significant shift away from the clinical area to education and management, particularly education (the category 'other' includes full-time courses, non-health care, family or missing data).

When respondents were asked about their future career the trend continued. 18% anticipated that they would be in clinical work (including community nursing), with 40% aiming for education jobs and 12% for management. 15% were in the 'other' category, and another 15% were 'don't knows'.

Comments on the questionnaire relating to career moves were analysed qualitatively, and provided some explanations for the quantitative results. Many respondents had taken the diploma course because they wanted to enter nurse education, using the course either for direct entry to a nurse tutor course or just as a 'prerequisite' or 'stepping stone' towards a teaching qualification. Sometimes the course was offered in conjunction with clinical teacher training.

Many others said that although they had started the diploma to improve or update their clinical practice, the course had decided them to go into teaching, so the diploma did prove to be a turning point in careers away from clinical and management posts. For example:

'The diploma pushed me away from management to education and research.'

One respondent said she looked towards education because of:

'A need for autonomy not fulfilled in clinical nursing.'

Others commented:

'The diploma increased awareness of education skills needed to promote changes in practice.'

Became aware of need for changes in attitudes which led to teaching career.'

With regard to diploma holders becoming involved in further studies, research etc., 63% of the sample had progressed to higher education (first and second degrees, other diploma courses, education certificates), 33% had engaged in research and 16% had had work published. Examples of the value of the diploma as a preparation for further study were cited in the comments. One student gained the confidence to apply for a district nurse course 'even though my age was against me'. Another took a psychology degree because she had enjoyed the subject so much on the diploma course. Several respondents commented on their ambition to proceed to a nursing degree.

Assumption 2

There was also interest in whether men would have more changes in career patterns than women. In fact, only 18% of men changed jobs compared to 61% of women but as Figure 4.2 shows, there is a more marked shift among men towards education and management after the diploma course. Twice as many women as men stay in clinical nursing and these number more than the women in the two other main areas. On the other hand, men outnumber women in education and management.

Again the trend continues when respondents were asked about their future career. In 5 years' time only 4% of men intended to be in clinical nursing compared to 23% of women. Of those currently engaged in further education courses, 35% were women and 59% were men.

All the differences between men and women respondents were statistically significant.

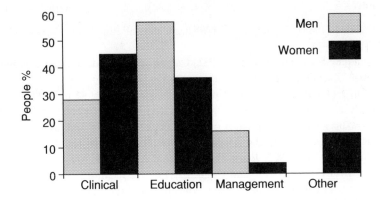

Figure 4.2 Careers after the diploma for men and women

Characteristics of the sample

The ratio of women to men in the sample was 77:23. The median age of respondents was 35 years. 75% of the sample were RGN/SRN qualified and 20% RMN (5% 'missing' or 'other'), the median year of basic qualification being 1976. 62% had at least one post-basic qualification and 10% had four. Nearly all were full-time employees.

Discussion

The results of the group research project were tending to confirm the two original assumptions. There were trends in the career patterns of the diploma students and these were stronger among the male respondents in the sample, yet some of the findings contradicted those from the literature. This study showed a drift away from clinical practice after diploma training, whereas other courses (Rogers, Montague and Herbert, Kemp) suggested that students remain clinicians. The explanation might be found in a comparison of age and experience. Because the nursing diploma courses are post-basic applicants tend to be mature, already have some years of experience and may be at a point of change. The sample indeed showed a mature range of ages from 27 to 56 years, with a variety of backgrounds, compared with the usual age of nursing graduates at the beginning of their careers. The comments made by respondents also lent support to this conclusion.

The findings on sex differences certainly supported those of Hardy, who found that male students outnumber females on nursing education courses. There were also parallels between our findings and Hardy's in terms of the number of students who go on to research activity.

References

1. Rogers J (1983) The impact of post-basic clinical education. *Nursing Times*, **79**(17): 42–44.
2. Montague S and Herbert R A (1982) Career paths of a degree-linked nursing course. *Journal of Advanced Nursing*, **7**: 359–370.
3. Kemp J (1985) The graduate's progress. *Nursing Times*, **81** (49): 42–43.
4. Hardy L K, Sinclair H and Hughes J (1984) Nursing careers: findings of a follow-up survey of graduates of the nursing education and administration certificate courses of the Department of Nursing Studies, University of Edinburgh, 1958–1975. *Journal of Advanced Nursing*, **9**: 611–618.
5. Sinclair H C, Hardy L K and Hughes J (1984) Educational achievements of nurses who completed the nursing education and the nursing administration certificate courses of the Department of Nursing Studies, University of Edinburgh 1958–1975. *Journal of Advanced Nursing*, **9**: 603–609.

CRITIQUE OF STUDY

Purpose of the research

Bedford *et al.* make it quite clear that this research was undertaken primarily as a student project, to provide a learning experience for a particular group of students. As such, rigour in the execution of the research could potentially have been sublimated at times to teaching needs. While this potential problem appears to have been overcome in the actual conduct of the research, the drawbacks of a consensus approach are apparent in some areas.

Development of research design and use of the literature

The initiation and development of the research was well explained, and the active participation of the course tutor ensured that there was adequate supervision at every stage. What was somewhat unusual was the way in which two assumptions were used as the basis for the research. More could have been made of the contradictions which were identified in the existing literature, and which could have led to the construction of a number of reasoned hypotheses. This feature is particularly surprising given the use of a questionnaire as the research tool, and the intention to employ statistical techniques for analysis. Such a research design lends itself admirably to hypothesis testing, and would have made more direct use of the statistical results.

Methodology

The sampling frame and sample were well constructed, and justified by the research aims. As this was a postal questionnaire the use of closed questions was sensible, while the inclusion of open questions provided respondents with the opportunity to express an opinion more fully.

What was lacking in the explanation of the method was why a control group was not used. What reasons were there for assuming that changes in the career pattern of diploma students were different from those of their contemporaries who did not take the diploma course? This seems a serious omission if the purpose of the research was to examine changes brought about by exposure to the experiences of the diploma course, and this does seem to be the case.

Presentation of results

The results presented are somewhat sparse, given that a tool as powerful as SPSS was used for the analysis. The labelling of Figure 4.1 does not make it entirely clear that each set of bars relates to the careers from which students on the diploma course came. This being so, the changes in careers which do indeed appear to have occurred could have been illustrated more clearly. The data presented concerning differences between men and women suffers from having no comparison with a control group. There is some evidence that male nurses as a group do aim their careers towards education and management.

Discussion

The explanation for the contradictions between the research findings and those of previous work is the greater degree of maturity of students undertaking the diploma course. What has not been clearly demonstrated is that the changes in career which were identified in diploma students were significantly different from those of nurses of similar maturity who did not take the diploma course.

Summary

The project presented was no doubt an invaluable learning exercise. The research was competently executed and resulted in some interesting findings. However, the limitations of the research design mean that it lacks reliability. However, the findings do provide several potentially fruitful avenues for further research.

EXERCISES

Now you have seen how the theory of a research critique is applied, see how well you get on with the exercises.

1. Choose a short paper and prepare a short critique on it, as if you were presenting it to a group of colleagues. Imagine that the presentation is to last no more than 10 minutes.
2. Choose a research-based paper and write a critique of approximately 1000 words. If possible it is best if the paper chosen is on an area of nursing with which you are familiar, as then you can approach the work with some degree of knowledge of the subject.

These two exercises are set at different levels of difficulty, so that you can become familiar with the techniques in the first exercise, then proceed to a more structured approach. In a group setting the short critique could be conducted by individuals and then presented and discussed in class, or two or three people could work together in preparing a critique for presentation and discussion with others.

FURTHER READING

Abdellah F and Levine C (1979) Analysis and interpretation of research findings. *Better Patient Care Through Nursing Research*, pp. 409–413. New York: Macmillan.

Chapman C C (1984) Evaluating published research. *The Research Process in Nursing*, ed. Cormack D F S. Oxford: Blackwell Scientific Publications.

Fox D J (1976) *Fundamentals of Research in Nursing*, 3rd edn, ch. 13. New York: Appleton-Century-Crofts.

Hawthorn P J (1983) Principles of research: a checklist, pp. 41–43. *Nursing Times* Occasional Paper, **79**(35): 41–43.

Hunt J (1984) Research: step by step. *Nursing Mirror*, **158**(1): 29–30.

Notter L (1979) The evaluation process. *Essentials of Research in Nursing*, ch. 11. London: Tavistock.

Treece E W and Treece J W (1986) Critiquing an article and critiquing skills. *Research in Nursing*, ch. 4. St Louis: Mosby.

Walker J (1984) Making sense of investigation. *Nursing Mirror*, **158**(10): 15–16.

5

Research Design

Research needs to be carefully planned if it is to have any credibility and usefulness. This planning process and the 'blueprint' to which it gives rise is known as the research design. Thinking about and planning the research design is a crucial stage in any project.

CHOOSING METHODS

Since the earliest development of nursing research there has been continuous debate as to whether quantitative or qualitative methods are the most appropriate. Early nurse researchers had no traditions or examples on which to build, so understandably turned to the natural sciences as a model. Also, if the new discipline was to be taken seriously then it had to be seen to be 'scientific' and 'respectable', so quantitative methods were concentrated upon.

One of the criticisms that used to be made of nursing research was that nursing had no theory-base of its own so had to 'borrow' from other disciplines, such as education, sociology or psychology. Why does this matter – is it not enough simply to gather the information required in order to answer the research question? The answer is that it is not that straightforward. As any nurse would point out, the difficulty is that nursing is not only a science. Carper (1978) identified four types of nursing knowledge:

1. Empirics – the science of nursing.
2. Aesthetics – the art of nursing.
3. Personal knowledge.
4. Ethics or moral knowledge.

Hockey (1986) described nursing as 'the art of applying nursing knowledge'. Nurses have been trying to define just what nursing is since Florence Nightingale's day, and will no doubt continue to do so. Clearly both art and science have to be taken into account, but what nurses do at any one time is likely to be somewhere along a continuum ranging from pure art to pure science. Similarly, nursing research can best be thought of not as qualitative *or* quantitative, but qualitative *and* quantitative. The diagram below illustrates this.

Art .... Science
Qualitative .... Quantitative

Where one is along these lines in both nursing and nursing research will depend on the purpose of the research and the experience, knowledge and clinical specialty of the person concerned.

At one end of the continuum are the studies that are purely about increasing knowledge. Examples of these would be studies of nurse–patient communication (Wells, 1980). At the other end of the continuum are the studies concerned mainly with suggesting and implementing changes in practice (Rodin, 1983). As we said earlier, however, theoretical research is intended to influence practice and practical research is based on theory. There is also research that combines both approaches. The various nursing models are examples of this. They generate nursing theory which is intended to guide nursing practice. You may also hear the terms 'basic' and 'applied' used to describe the two approaches.

Weiss (1977) wrote about the nature of research which attempts to influence policy. He distinguished between decision-driven and knowledge-driven models of policy research. Although decision-driven research is often specifically commissioned to aid decision making, knowledge-driven research, while more theoretical, is often more influential on policy change in the long term.

Nurse researchers need to beware, therefore, of being forced to accept the policy-makers' definition of the problem and to supply preconceived answers. Research should involve a degree of academic freedom; thus the nurse researcher needs to keep in touch with theoretical bases and be continually challenging and negotiating.

Nursing as a discipline draws knowledge from a wide range of sources, each with its own style of research. The potential choice of research styles and methods for nursing research is therefore very wide, ranging from the highly quantitative methods of the biological and medical sciences through the social sciences and humanities to more qualitative methods. This relates to the art–science continuum described earlier.

Quantitative methods .... Qualitative methods
Biological and
medical sciences .... Social sciences .... Humanities

Quantitative research is concerned primarily with measurement of facts – about people, events or things and establishing the strength of the relationship between variables, usually by statistical tests. Large-scale research on groups of people, all nurses who qualified in a certain year and their subsequent career patterns, for example, would use quantitative methods to collect large amounts of data, but small research projects may also be best conducted in this way. The theory behind quantitative research is that only by employing such methods can confidence be placed in the results. Quantitative research is sometimes described as providing 'hard' data.

Qualitative research, on the other hand, is based on the rationale that human behaviour can only be understood by getting to know the perspective and interpretation of events of the person or people being studied – by seeing things through their eyes, rather than by reliance on the measurement of concrete facts. In this it follows the tradition of anthropologists and sociologists. Qualitative methods may be used for a complete study or may be used before a quantitative study (e.g. a survey) or after a quantitative study (to explain a statistical relationship). Qualitative research is described as providing 'soft' data.

FIT OF THEORY AND METHOD

Research, nursing or otherwise, at its simplest level aims to answer a question. As related and similar questions are examined and illustrated so they begin to fit together into a broader pattern known as a theory. Whatever the research design and no matter where on the research spectrum, the work will be strengthened and enhanced if it is related to an appropriate theoretical framework. The theoretical basis of a piece of research guides the formulation of an hypothesis, indicates the type of data required and hence the most suitable methodology and provides a means of interpreting and understanding the data collected. Whereas research which is not related to theory may provide interesting information, it cannot contribute to the wider body of knowledge as there is no context. The explanation that appears to fit the data best is limited to that study and is not generalisable.

Theories develop from systematic formal research, which provides an increasing body of knowledge about the complex relationships between people and their environment. Theory is classified as *inductive* or *deductive*.

Inductive theory
particular case
(observed data) ⟶ testable hypothesis ⟶ generalised
theory

Deductive theory
generalised
theory ⟶ testable hypothesis ⟶ particular case

This illustration suggests that inductive and deductive theory are two distinct phenomena, but this is definitely not the case. Inductive reasoning may be used to explain why certain things occurred – if some patients comply with the medication prescribed for them and some do not, a theory about 'self' from psychology may explain the difference. The theory may then be used deductively to suggest how other patients may behave – diabetic patients' compliance with diet, for example. Theories can describe, explain, predict or prescribe.

Theory used to describe

If you remember from the 'getting started' chapter, one of the questions posed was 'what is going on here?'. Much research is descriptive in that it seeks to answer that type of question. Once the research has been conducted, a particular theory may help to interpret the findings by describing in a structured way just what is happening. For example, in her study of nurse–patient communication in surgical wards Macleod Clark (1983) considered that the limited nature of the conversations analysed could best be understood in relation to nurses' tendency to distance themselves from patients.

Theory used to explain

Although describing a situation may be sufficient in some contexts, often there is a need to look for the reason behind the situation. Theory can provide an explanation; for instance, Bond (1983) used theories related to non-disclosure of their condition to patients suffering from cancer to explain the way nurses 'managed' the nurse–patient interaction.

Theory used to predict

As well as providing an explanation of why things happen, theories can also predict what will happen given a specific set of circumstances. Some research sets out to test whether a particular prediction holds good.

In an experimental design, Webb (1983) predicted from existing theory concerning coping mechanisms that women given an information and support counselling session following hysterectomy would recover more quickly and be more satisfied with their care.

Theory used to prescribe

As we have said before in this book, one of the criticisms of nursing research and of nursing as a discipline is that it has no true theory of its own. If you look back to the earlier chapters, one of the reasons for getting involved in research is to provide a basis for rational decisions about the care given to patients. Theory can and should be used to decide just what nursing care will be the most effective. For instance, educational theory may be employed by the nurse to decide what form a teaching programme for renal patients being dialysed should take if it is to succeed. Theories concerning stress and coronary heart disease can guide the nurse in the information given to those attending a well-person clinic. Utilising research findings in this way is perhaps the biggest challenge facing nursing today.

How does this affect research design? The point is that at the design stage, in fact even before that, the question to be answered is whether to develop or utilise a theory and then collect data which seeks to support it, or to collect data first and then try to develop a theory to fit, or to adapt existing theory. Clearly, if you are trying to test theory which seems relevant to your particular subject of interest then you will set out to collect the kind of data which will verify or refute that theory (prediction). On the other hand, if you collect the data first then the limitations of the data and the kind of data you collect will itself, to some extent, dictate the range of theory which will fit your particular data (description or explanation). Theory may guide the method, but the method will limit or control the resulting theory.

As in many aspects of research there is no clear-cut answer. Theory both precedes and follows research. It precedes by guiding the thinking on the factors which are important to investigate in research. It follows because it helps to set the research in the context of other research. Consequently, it both indicates the research direction and shows how isolated findings relate to the more abstract body of knowledge. Research, then, can both originate from and contribute to theory.

Glaser and Strauss (1967) have written extensively on grounded theory, which is theory derived from and verified by the data in a continuous process. As explanatory theory begins to emerge, data is collected which will support, refute or refine. This is arguably more credible than explaining data arising from one research enterprise by theory originating from another.

Nurses are beginning to develop theories of nursing, but must not fall into the trap of taking these theories as sacrosanct. As a mature discipline nursing must have the confidence to put theory to the test.

The continuum between quantitative and qualitative methods can be represented by the three main research styles:

Quantitative .... Qualitative
Experiment .... Survey .... Interpretative

EXPERIMENTAL METHODS

In an experiment, measurement is made under conditions of sytematic control of different features (variables) of a research setting.

Not all experiments are carried out by white-coated men in laboratories. There are different kinds of experimental designs, but the simplest way of thinking about it is the classic 'before and after' model. A sample of patients is chosen and measurements on some variables are taken – knowledge of their special diet requirements, for example. Then some manipulation takes place – a teaching programme, for instance, and the measurement repeated. The aim of the experiment would be to see whether the patients' knowledge of diet was improved by planned teaching.

Advantages: Strong conclusions can be drawn about the cause and effect of the variables under study.

Disadvantages: Experiments cannot usually be performed in a social setting. They are therefore conducted in 'artificial' situations which may not appear to relate to the 'real' world. There are also ethical issues to be considered in all experiments.

SURVEY METHODS

These use questionnaires, tests and interviews with large samples of the population under study. This approach is sometimes called *Descriptive research* because it describes what is going on.

Advantages: Information can be collected quickly and comparatively cheaply.

Disadvantages: The information may be superficial.

INTERPRETATIVE METHODS

These use observations and interviews in natural settings. Towell's work (1975) on psychiatric nursing is a classic example of this.

Advantages: Produces in-depth data on the interpretations of the research setting by participants.

Disadvantages: Time consuming. Over-identification by researcher with research setting. Findings may not be generalisable.

These are, of course, only broad definitions. Variations and combinations of the styles exist along the continuum. In addition, there are some some other methods that do not neatly fit into these categories. Although it is unlikely that you would want to use them when you are starting out in research, it is useful to know a little about such methods in case you come across examples when you are reading research papers. For convenience we have called these *alternative methods*.

ALTERNATIVE METHODS

Historical research

Medical and nursing knowledge is constantly changing and developing. At first glance, therefore, it would seem that historical research is a waste of time, but this is definitely not so. For some research questions it is impossible to decide what is happening now and what may happen in the future without looking at what has happened in the past. Understanding the reasons behind the present situation can provide vital clues about the effect of and attitudes to future plans or policies. This is particularly true of more 'social' issues such as attitudes to the elderly or handicapped.

Case and life histories

Asking people to relate things that happened to them at certain periods of their life can help to build up a picture of the conditions that existed at the time and how people felt about them. By examining a number of such histories more comprehensive conclusions about the social policies in operation, what led to them and their consequences can be drawn.

Coming from 'those who were there', the technique provides very rich data; however, as you will have realised, the big problem with such data is the accuracy of recall if the account is retrospective, as it usually is. There is less of a problem if the research is conducted as events occur, but it still places a great deal of reliance on the version of events given by those relating their 'histories'.

Use of documents

Documents may enable you to verify the verbal accounts given in a case history but can be used alone as a source of data. At a personal level letters, diaries, engagement books and address books can be useful. Public documents include newspapers, magazines, committee minutes, reports, official statements and press releases. It is better to trace the original source of such documents if possible, as a first-hand account is more accurate than hearsay.

Content analysis

This is really a particular way of using documents. There are two methods of doing this:

1. Counting the number of times a particular variable is mentioned in certain documents. Mentions in newspapers of shortage of nursing staff is a good example.
2. The content or manner in which a variable is treated in particular documents. For example, has sexual stereotyping, or aspects to this in newspapers, changed over time?

All the documents mentioned above can be subjected to content analysis. Which you choose will depend on the purpose of the research. The data can be analysed quantitatively if you are using the first method discussed, or qualitatively if the latter. Analysing quantitative and qualitative data will be discussed in later chapters.

Critical incidents

There are three types of critical incident material:

1. Such things as accident and incident reports or staff and patient complaints. If there was an increased number of patient accidents from a particular ward, then there is clearly an indication that all is not well. By examining such information, perhaps comparing one clinical area with another, trends over time or precipitating causes, the researcher may be able to draw some conclusions about the area under study.
2. Another technique is to ask people to rank a list of events in order of importance. Is making the beds more important to a nurse than talking to a distressed patient, or less so? By asking a number of respondents to rank the same list the researcher can gain some idea of the value system and attitudes in the area being studied.
3. By asking people to describe certain events that were particularly successful or unsuccessful, it is possible to analyse just what it was about the way the event occurred that made it a success – or failure. For example, after asking mothers recently delivered what they felt was particularly good about the event, the researcher would be able to identify things that the midwives could do to make more deliveries successful – telling the mother exactly what was happening, giving lots of encouragement, for instance. This is known as Flanagan's Critical Incident Technique (Norman *et al.*, 1992).

Delphi system

The Ancient Greeks used to go to Delphi to consult the oracle. Fortunately the Delphi technique does not require a trip to Greece – but it is about consulting experts. This is done by inviting a panel of experts (by post) to give their opinion on a particular issue, perhaps by ranking items in order of importance, an attitude scale of some kind or giving their opinion. The results are analysed and returned to each member of the panel (although in a non-attributable manner). Then they are asked to complete a new instrument generated from the findings of the first round. The second time they will, of course, know how others on the panel responded and may modify their answers in the light of this. This analysis and response may be repeated up to four times, the aim being to arrive at a consensus of expert opinion. The advantage of this method is that you can gain the views of experts whom it may be difficult to interview individually. The disadvantage is that it can be costly in stationery and postage and how up to date are the experts anyway?

Computer modelling

This very sophisticated method requires a great deal of computer expertise to conduct. The researcher sets up on a computer a 'model' of a particular set of variables interacting in a certain relationship; then one or other of the variables is changed and the effect on the others measured. The management accountants who advised the UKCC on Project 2000 used this technique to examine the effect on the number of nurses which was likely to result from certain events: a change of entry requirements, for example, or a different percentage of non-practising nurses returning to the NHS. The advantage of the method is that it enables the researcher to set up situations and test out relationships and hypotheses in a way which would be difficult, if not impossible, in real life. The disadvantage, as with all computer usage, is that if you put rubbish in you get rubbish out!

Game simulation

The intention behind game simulation is that in setting up some form of game – perhaps role play – people will respond in the same way as they would in real life. It is difficult to prove to what extent this is true and such games need very careful handling on the part of the researcher if they are not to cause great distress and anxiety to the participants. If you have ever taken part in this sort of exercise as part of a course you will no doubt recognise the problem from your own experience. On the other hand, it may be the only way to gain access to certain situations.

One-way mirrors

Clearly, there are very real ethical problems with this method, so the benefits expected to result from such a project should be clear and unambiguous. One-way mirrors are sometimes used to assess a child's reaction to certain stimuli, or how the child interacts with toys or with others. As with game simulation, it may be the only way to get near to the actual behaviour or attitudes under study.

It is not a question of 'which method should I use?' but rather one of 'which research approach is most suitable for my research question?', and then 'what research technique is most likely to give me the data (information) that I need?' (Figure 5.1). The question of whether to use qualitative or quantitative methods will be largely resolved by thinking first about the research approach and techniques which are most appropriate. If the research is of an exploratory nature, trying to find out what is going on in a given situation, then quantitative techniques such as a structured questionnaire would not be appropriate. There may be very little literature on the subject, so theories which will form the framework may not be valid or may contain unsubstantiated assumptions. Quantitative research looks to existing theory in deducing the likely explanation in the relationship between variables which the research sets out to establish.

Qualitative research, by focusing on respondents' perspectives, formulates theories, explanations and hypotheses during and after data collection by induction. The theory thus evolved is relevant to the specific time and setting of the research study. Research which aims to find out about attitudes – how nurses feel about caring for the dying for example – requires qualitative methods, perhaps interviews.

Later chapters will discuss the methods listed above in more detail, but you can see from Figure 5.1 how the method must flow from the approach which is most suitable to the research question, rather than be an isolated decision based on personal preference and narrow thinking.

Whichever approach and techniques are chosen the researcher must bear in mind the *validity, reliability* and *reactivity* of the research methods finally applied.

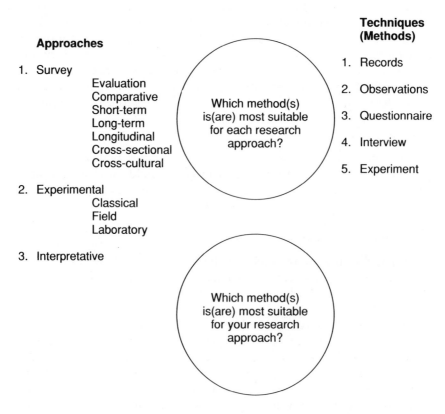

Figure 5.1 Approach-method relationships in research

VALIDITY

There are several different kinds and meanings of validity, but it is easiest to think of them as either *internal validity* or *external validity*.

Internal validity

Internal validity is about the measurement tools themselves. Are they measuring what you think they are measuring? Is the data you are collecting a 'true' picture of what is happening? A good example of a test that lacks validity is the early intelligence tests. After some years of using these as an indication of the intellectual ability of children it was realised that as the tests relied heavily on the meanings and relationships of words they were really testing the pupils' understanding of the English language. Questionnaires can be more of a test of memory and the ability to recall events than a data collection method about a specific subject. Even seemingly tried and tested methods can lack validity – how close is the agreement on a blood pressure reading taken by 10 different nurses?

External Validity

External validity concerns the appropriateness of the measurement tools to answer the research question. If you want to find out the feelings of a residents' association to a new community home for the mentally handicapped, would an attitude scale really show what they thought and more importantly, how they would behave?

RELIABILITY

In research language *reliability* refers to the extent to which your findings can be generalised to other settings.

Reliability is a factor on two levels; time and place. First, if a questionnaire or other research tool was applied on a particular day would the same result be obtained if the same method was applied at a later date to the same research sample? Secondly, could the research tools be used with similar results in another place? If so, then the findings of the research are applicable elsewhere.

REACTIVITY

However carefully set up, all research, even an experiment, takes place in a social context. That is, people are required to interact with each other and with the setting and objects around them, so researcher and subjects will be reacting to each other's presence and behaviour. The extent to which this influences the research data is known as *reactivity*.

Suppose you were interviewed about your views on the wards you have worked on: your answers might well be different if the questioner was one of the ward sisters than those you might give to someone unconnected with the hospital. It has been shown, for instance, that subjects respond in a different way to male researchers than to females.

Another way in which reactivity can occur is in the researcher's influence on the research situation itself, or the data collected. In an interview, for example, if the researcher appears shocked or ignores some things the respondent says, the latter will probably not mention these again. The researcher has therefore made some choices about what information is collected and equally what is not, perhaps even without realising it. If the method being used involves the researcher as a participant, then his or her actions will inevitably have some effect on the situation under study.

So far we have talked about choosing one research approach and one method. However, there is another type of research design called *triangulation*.

You may have seen triangulation markers at the tops of hills or other landmarks. These are obtained by taking sightings of the point from more than one direction, then marking where they meet. Triangulation in research means very much the same thing. The research question is tackled by different approaches, by a variety of methods, and perhaps by even more than one theory. This serves two main purposes. First, it helps to confirm the results obtained in any one method. Secondly, by looking at the problem from another research approach a different perspective can be brought to bear on the topic under investigation. Thus the results can be treated with more confidence, and a wider range of explanatory theory used and tested. Hopefully, greater illumination of the subject will be achieved.

In designing your research, then, choose the approach which is the most appropriate for the questions you wish to answer. This, not methodological dogma, should always be the primary concern in any research.

SCENARIO

Qualitative versus quantitative

It has been agreed that Staff Nurse Baker should undertake an evaluation of the change to a 5-day ward, but in discussions with the rest of the ward team on what form this evaluation should take it becomes clear that members of staff hold varying opinions on the matter.

Sister Hudson has always been more interested in the scientific component of nursing. She considers her decisions as ward manager are based on rational arguments and carefully proven facts. Her view is that the evaluation should concentrate on collecting very specific information which will, she assumes, speak for itself. Besides, Sister considers that the hospital managers will only take facts and figures seriously. However, although personal inclination and talents are bound to play a part in research design, they are by no means the overriding factor.

The community nurse, Sister Brown, points out that though sound reasoning and clear evidence is necessary, people are too complex and their actions too complicated to reduce to a set of numbers and display of tables. How will patients feel about the new policy? If patients or their relatives are not able to cope with earlier discharge then that will have an effect on her work. Student Nurse Green has heard a little about qualitative research in the research module she has just finished. Staff Nurse Baker agrees with Sister about the need to be scientific, but wonders whether some kind of experiment is possible. After all, the whole point of experiments is to prove things, surely?

Discussions about what kind of research to carry out and which methods are more reliable become quite heated at times! What the team are forgetting is that the decision about the approach to use must be made taking into account the purpose of the research, and what would be the most appropriate approach to achieve that. One aspect of this debate is whether the research is to be qualitative or quantitative in character.

So what would be the best approach for evaluating the new ward policy?

One aspect which will need to be studied is the number of patients likely to be affected by the change. From this it will be possible to deduce how this will change the work-load of the ward. One way of doing this would be to look at records of past operation lists, a historical approach using quantitative methods to provide the data required.

The question of whether patients, who are discharged from hospital soon after operation, will take more time to care for at home, requires a different approach. Not only do the specific types of nursing procedures need to be examined, but psychological and emotional support such as counselling and teaching must be considered.

While a survey of patients referred to the community nurses would enable the time required to be worked out, it will not help the community nurse to know how much patients are likely to know about their illness or how their families manage. A survey of patients referred over a specified time period would give quantitative data on which to base estimates of work-load and types of care needed, while interviews with a sample of patients who are in hospital for 5 days or less would provide qualitative data on how patients feel about being discharged fairly quickly from hospital and how much they know about their condition. A semi-structured questionnaire will be best as then more open-ended questions can be included, enabling patients to explain how they feel about the situation. This phase of the research will employ a descriptive approach.

As interviews are to be conducted with patients the consent of the Ethical Committee will have to be sought.

Another aspect of the research is to compare the ward's existing nursing records with a new set intended for the 5-day policy. In deciding how to go about this the team must decide what questions they want answered. Do they want to know whether the new notes take longer to complete? If so, then structured non-participant observation would be appropriate in an open context. Or do they wish to find out if nurses are able to use the new notes more easily to refer to in caring for patients? In this case, participant observation in a closed context might provide better data. Alternatively, the team might be more concerned with the opinions of staff and patients about the new notes.

These could best be sought in interviews, but then people would have to be asked about the old notes as well, otherwise how can the two be compared? Interviews will mean obtaining the permission of senior managers and if patients are involved, the Ethical Committee again. In the end the team decide they want to see if the new notes are easier to refer to in the day to day care of patients, so plans are made to set up an experimental situation using the old notes on one half of the ward and the new notes on the other.

For each question to be answered a different research approach and the appropriate methodology are required. Good research is when the best fit between these two is achieved.

Exercises

1. Write down all the research methods you can remember having heard about. Your list should include some of these:
   Questionnaires
   Interviews
   Observation
   Using records and documents
   Attitude scales
2. Imagine you are one of the team on Ward 4. What questions concerning the change to a 5-day ward do you think could be answered by research, and what approach and method do you think would be most appropriate? Then think of all the factors of validity, reliability and reactivity which must be considered, and how they might be overcome.
3. In class, or with a group of friends, discuss the difference between a nursing theory and a theory for nursing. In what kinds of research would each be relevant?

REFERENCES

Bond S (1983) Nurses' communication with cancer patients. In: Wilson-Barnett J (ed), *Nursing Research, Ten Studies in Patient Care*. Chichester: Wiley.

Carper B A (1978) Fundamental patterns of knowing in nursing. *Advances in Nursing Science*, **1**. In: Ackerman W B and Lohnes P R, *Research Methods for Nurses*. New York: McGraw Hill.

Glaser B and Strauss A (1967) *The Discovery of Grounded Theory: Strategies for Qualitative Research*. Chicago: Aldine.

Hockey L (1986) Nursing Research: its pleasures, problems and potential for nursing. Paper presented at Wessex Regional Research Conference at Dorset Institute of Higher Education, Poole, 29 November 1986.

Macleod Clark J (1983) Nurse–patient communication: an analysis of conversations from surgical wards. In: Wilson-Barnett J (ed), *Nursing Research, Ten Studies in Patient Care*. Chichester: Wiley.

Norman I *et al.* (1992) Developing Flanagan's Critical Incident Technique to elicit indicators of high and low quality nursing care from patients and their nurses. *Journal of Advanced Nursing*, **17**: 590–600.

Rodin J (1983) Preparing children in hospital. In: Wilson-Barnett J (ed), *Nursing Research: Ten studies in Patient Care*. Chichester: Wiley.

Towell D (1975) *Understanding Psychiatric Nursing: a Sociological Study of Modern Psychiatric Nursing Practice*. London: Royal College of Nursing.

Webb C (1983) A study of recovery from hysterectomy. In: Wilson-Barnett J (ed), *Nursing Research, Ten Studies in Patient Care*. Chichester: Wiley.

Weiss C H (ed.) (1977) *Using Social Research in Public Policy Making*. Mass: Lexington Books.

Wells T (1980) *Problems in Geriatric Care: a Study of Nurses' Problems in Care of Old People in Hospitals*. Edinburgh: Churchill Livingstone.

FURTHER READING

Fox D J (1976) Research approaches. *Fundamentals of Research in Nursing*, 3rd edn, ch. 9. New York: Appleton-Century-Crofts.

Hockey L (1979) Indicators in nursing research with emphasis on social indicators. *Journal of Advanced Nursing*, **2** (3): 239–250.

Macleod Clark J and Hockey L (1981) Overview of research design and methods. *Research for Nursing: a Guide for the Enquiring Nurse*, ch. 2. London: H M and M Publishers.

McFarlane J (1977) Developing a theory of nursing: the relation of theory, practice, education and research. *Journal of Advanced Nursing*, **2** (3): 261–270.

Polit D and Hungler B (1985) Principles of research design. *Essentials of Nursing Research*, ch. 8. Philadelphia: J B Lippincott.

Treece E W and Treece J W (1986) Reliability and validity. *Elements of Research in Nursing*, ch. 15. St Louis: Mosby.

6

Experimental Methods

You may decide that an experimental approach is most appropriate for your research because it offers the possibility of establishing links between change and its consequences with 'hard' quantitative data. Experimental methods are about finding causal connections, usually through comparison of different groups or states, by following strict logical rules. We can be reasonably confident about the results because measurements are made under controlled conditions. The results can be helpful in understanding why things happen and predicting future events. Statistical tests have been designed to check whether any differences shown in the results are due to the intervention or simply chance (see Chapter 9 on analysing data).

We should remember, however, that numbers can give a false sense of security. Unless we are studying under strict laboratory conditions there will always be some doubt about the variability of measurements, especially if the study is of variable, fallible human beings in natural surroundings!

In the last chapter we described the three main styles of experiment, survey and interpretative research. We have chosen to start with experiments in this chapter, continuing our discussion of which methods to choose in research design. This is not because we are particularly recommending experimental design, as all methods have a value in answering research questions. It really depends on the question. We are starting with the experiment because it is at one end of the continuum of methods deriving from different theoretical perspectives in nursing, the most structured and quantitative end. It represents the purest form of scientific enquiry discussed in Chapter 1. In the following chapters we will cover the main styles in turn so that they can be compared with each other, until we reach the other end of the continuum, the qualitative methods, which represent a reaction to the scientific tradition.

DEFINITIONS

Experimental methods are quite familiar at an everyday level, in the idea of the classic 'before and after' design and in health care as the basis for much medical research, such as drug trials. The method is used in nursing as, for example, in the classic studies by Hayward (1975) and Boore (1978), where patients' responses to pain after pre-operative information were compared with the responses of those receiving routine treatment. The principles of experimental design are also applied in evaluation and action research so current in the climate of quality assurance in the health services today, and will be dealt with later in the chapter.

Let us try to define the experiment precisely to see how it can be applied to solve problems in nursing practice. Colin Robson gives a straightforward definition in his book, *Experiment, Design and Statistics in Psychology* (1973):

'In an experiment, one investigates the relationship between two (or more) things by deliberately producing a change in one of them and looking at, observing the change in the other. These "things" in which change takes place are usually called variables.'

The word 'variable' simply means something that can vary – a characteristic of a person or object that varies, can be observed and can be measured.

Experiments are therefore extremely relevant to assessing changes in nursing practice and nursing services generally. If a new medication for pressure sores were introduced, for instance, we would be interested to see if the rate of healing varied compared to other treatments. Experimental design could help us to do this accurately. At another level, experimental design has been used to compare the quality of life of residents in a long-stay hospital with those in new community units.

The convention for studying variables in experiments is to identify them as independent and dependent variables. The *independent* variable is the one that we manipulate deliberately to produce change. In our example above the treatment for pressure sores is the independent variable. In the case of the comparison of hospital and community care, the independent variable is the model of care.

It follows that the *dependent* variable is the one we look at for change.

Now that we have begun to explore what experimental design means, we can develop the ideas by looking at some more complicated definitions of experiments. An Open University course on social research methods defines the experiment as:

'measurement under conditions of systematic control of different features of the research setting' (Open University, 1984)

A Dictionary of Social Science Methods says:

> 'A study undertaken to test one or more hypotheses and in which the relevant variables are controlled and manipulated by the experimenter, rather than simply observed in their natural setting.' (Miller and Wilson, 1983)

These quotations introduce two further points: that experiments follow from hypotheses and the question of control of variables. A further consideration is that of ethics when applying principles of experimental design to human individuals. We shall be dealing with these points in the following sections.

HYPOTHESIS

We mentioned hypothesis in the first and second chapters. An hypothesis offers a possible explanation for a research problem. Sometimes it is simply stated as a question. The point about an hypothesis is that it is a clear statement of the likely outcome of an experiment, which the researcher will either support or reject. The rejection of the hypothesis is also anticipated at the outset and expressed as a 'null hypothesis'. This is a convention in the statistical testing of results that will be explained in more detail later and in Chapter 9. To take one of our earlier examples, the hypothesis might be:

> 'Residents in a community home have more contacts with their relatives than residents in a long-stay hospital.'

Whereas the null hypothesis would say:

> 'Residents in a community home have no more contacts with their relatives than residents in a long-stay hospital.'

In the scientific approach, writing an hypothesis is the next stage after the initial statement of the research problem and a review of the literature. It is central to theory building, where every new idea is tested rigorously to add to our knowledge about the world and in turn stimulates further investigation. The hypothesis should predict the relationship between the independent and dependent variables in a way that can be measured. The statement of the problem needs to be successively refined and narrowed, therefore, so that the focus is on the main variables, how they can be researched and the likely outcome of their association or the effect of changes in one on the other. This may generate more than one hypothesis. If we take the example from Chapter 2 where we arrived at the statement of a problem as:

> 'Can non-verbal communication be used effectively by nurses as a

means of initiating leisure activities with adults with a profound mental handicap in a residential setting?'

we could express this in the form of at least four separate hypotheses for testing:

1. Nurses vary in their use of non-verbal skills with clients.
2. The greater the use of non-verbal skills by nurses, the more effective they are in initiating activities with clients.
3. Clients will vary in their responsiveness to non-verbal skills.
4. Training staff in the use of non-verbal skills will increase their effectiveness with clients in initiating activities.

The literature review helps in the refining of a problem statement into an hypothesis and this is why one should continue reading in parallel to the design stage of a research study.

The exploratory stages of a study will also assist in deciding how to convert or operationalise ideas in the statement into observable, measurable variables. In our example of pressure sores, the effectiveness of medication on the pressure sore could be measured by the speed of healing in terms of time, by changes in size or by any other observable signs.

A good hypothesis, therefore, will suggest the design for a research study that would attempt to prove or disprove its predictions. Hypothesis allows for the possibility that there will be no effect between the independent and the dependent variables. Statistical tests used with experimental data are based on the principle of the null hypothesis – that there is no relationship expected between the variables – so if their measurement does show a related variation that is taken as a significant result.

We cannot really talk about 'proof' in such absolute terms, however. Results of experimental studies are usually worded more tentatively, talking of how results 'support' or 'tend to confirm' the hypothesis.

CONTROL OF VARIABLES

If a teacher wanted to try a new way of teaching, for instance, exercises rather than lectures as the means of teaching research methods, how could the results of the new approach be evaluated? First, if the new approach were to be checked in a fairly scientific way, an hypothesis would be needed. For example:

Exercises are a more successful way of teaching research methods to nursing students than lectures.

The simplest evaluation would be a type of case study where the results of the group learning by the new approach could be measured in some way. This can be represented in diagrammatic form as shown in Figure 6.1.

Independent variable (IV)	Dependent variable (DV)
Teaching research by exercises	Group's response

Time ─────────────────────▶

Figure 6.1 Simple design for measuring effects of the independent variable

The independent variable is the new teaching approach but could represent any intervention or change. The dependent variable here is the effect on the group of students.

Exercise

How could the dependent variable be operationalised and measured in this example?

Discussion
Various measures could be used to assess the success of different teaching approaches. The conventional means, of course, are exams and assignments to test students' knowledge of remembered facts. Other methods could include asking students to rate the new approach, seeing how much time it took to cover the topics, or simply counting how many students fell asleep!

Exercise

Can you see any problems with the case study method as an experimental design?

Discussion
You might have mentioned that it would be more sensible to compare the effects of the two teaching approaches, which, in diagrammatic form, would look something like Figure 6.2.

Sometimes, it is possible to try two different types of intervention on the same group and compare the results. In our example it might be all right to compare *teaching* by lectures or exercises with the same group if we were measuring something like students' alertness or sleepiness.

IV	DV
Lectures	Group's response
Exercises	Group's response

Time ————————————————————→

Figure 6.2 Design for comparing two versions of the independent variable

However, if we wanted to check *learning* on a specific topic, we would have to use two groups – (a different group for each of the two methods, otherwise the learning from whichever method was used to start with would affect the learning from the method which followed. In this case it would be vital to match the two groups so that they were similar in most respects, to be sure that any differences in student performance were due to the different teaching approaches.

Another important point might be what the group or groups were like beforehand. If we were checking something such as knowledge, this would need to be assessed before and after the intervention of the independent variable (the teaching approach) (Figure 6.3).

DV	IV	DV
Group's knowledge	Teaching approach	Group's knowledge

Time ————————————————————→

Figure 6.3 Design for measuring before and after the introduction of the independent variable

DV	IV	DV
Control group's response	Lectures	Control group's response
Experimental group's response	Exercises	Experimental group's response

Time ──────────────────►

Figure 6.4 Before-and-after design with control group for comparison

EXPERIMENTAL DESIGN

Combining the two considerations we arrive at the classic experimental before-and-after design with an experimental group and a control group (Figure 6.4).

With this design we can more confidently compare differences in performance (whatever the measure used) to see if they support the hypothesis that teaching research methods by exercises is a more effective approach. More complex designs can be used with more than two groups or with several controlled dependent and independent variables.

Exercise

In our example of the tutor teaching research methods, can you see any other problems in comparing the two different teaching groups?

Discussion
As we have already observed, there may be other factors than the identified independent variable that could influence the outcome of the different teaching approaches.

Even if the groups were matched as far as possible in terms of age, sex, race, ability and so on, there might be differences in the conditions in which the classes took place. Did the classes happen in the same place, in the same room? Did they have the same teacher? If the groups were taught in different years or on different days, were there other events happening that might have made a difference? For instance, in one year a gloomy economic or political mood may exist as a backdrop to all activities. Fridays might have a different atmosphere to Mondays. Timing is obviously also important. The events such as other lessons that precede the research teaching might influence students' receptiveness. If we are using the number of students who fall asleep as an indicator, lessons after lunch are notoriously soporific!

If the student group were more sleepy in a lecture session after lunch than the other group in a morning session of exercises we could not necessarily conclude that the lecture was less successful, because there are other variables such as time of day operating as competing independent variables. These are called uncontrolled, extraneous or confounding variables. The only way to achieve a true comparison would be to compare two different teaching sessions under as similar conditions as possible. It would be interesting to compare two post-lunch sessions, for example, to see if fewer people fell asleep in the exercise session as hypothesised.

Our example here has demonstrated what was meant in the earlier definition of the experiment as 'systematic control of different features of the research setting' and 'relevant variables are controlled and manipulated by an experimenter'. Unless potentially confounding variables are controlled they could systematically bias the results, so that in manipulating the independent variable the experimenter might inadvertently manipulate other things at the same time. We need to be sure that the effects on the dependent variable are due to the chosen independent variable. There can also be problems with the measurement of the dependent variable, and particular attention needs to be paid to the validity and reliability of the measures, as discussed in the previous chapter. Control of variables is critical if one is looking for causal connections between the variables. The rules for establishing causality are:

1. There must be evidence of an association between the variable/s and the dependent variable/s (conventionally called X and Y).
2. X must be prior in time to Y.
3. No other variable can explain the effects on Y, otherwise the effect could be called 'spurious'. The association between smoking and lung cancer has also been called spurious because both could be caused by other psychosocial factors.

SUMMARY

We conclude this section with a summary of the discussion on the logic and definitions of experiments:

1. In the most basic form of the experiment, a chosen group is given an experimental treatment that is systematically controlled.
2. A control group, which is chosen in the same way from the same

population, does not receive the experimental treatment, but all other conditions are the same.

3. The treatment that is changed is called the independent variable.
4. Both groups are assessed on some outcome measure that is the dependent variable.
5. If the groups differ on the dependent variable, the conclusion is that the change in the independent variable had caused the difference and the hypothesis is confirmed.
6. Alternative explanations for the differences are controlled for by ensuring that the groups are equivalent in all respects except for the one being tested.

QUASI-EXPERIMENTS

Although the classic before-and-after design shown in Figure 6.4 is the ideal for experiments, the other designs illustrated are also viable and may be the only option in natural settings. It is here that experiment becomes more *quasi-experiment*. For instance, there may only be data available for one group or the only groups that can be compared have not been matched. Cook and Campbell's book on quasi-experimentation (1979) provides some useful statistical tactics to compensate for the lack of rigour in design.

ETHICS

The appeal of experimental methods, as we have seen, is their potential to determine facts and links between them. Most of us experience serious reservations however, about the application of experimental methods to people. Experiments on rats, for example, show a link between smoking and cancer, but this cannot be replicated ethically on human subjects. Some would say that the methods are also unethical on animals.

The rigour of experimental control can clash with social and professional values such as care and concern for the individual, maintenance and the preservation of life. It is not ethical, for instance, for a nurse to withhold treatment from a group just for the sake of comparing that group with another. We cannot make patients or clients suffer in the name of research.

The ethical issues surrounding research are examined more fully in Chapter 10. We want here to quote some examples of experimental research in nursing where the researcher may have had to compromise on scientific rigour to keep within professional codes of conduct. Most such studies compare a new intervention with the existing one, or offer different interventions to each group rather than deny the control group treatment. In an experimental study of touch by midwives to alleviate anxiety in women in labour (Lorenson, 1983), the control group were still given routine treatment. Some dubious practices still exist, however. In a comparison of family planning methods, the difference between groups was measured by unplanned pregnancies! Whereas the volunteers were said to be willing, it does seem unethical to ask a group to try a contraceptive with unknown risks and possible long-term side effects on their lives.

The medical profession has helped to establish some ground rules through its tradition of drug trial research and all proposed health-service research involving patients must now be submitted to a local committee for scrutiny. The operation of ethical committees is discussed in more detail in the next chapter.

EVALUATION AND ACTION RESEARCH

This section considers the application of experimental or quasi-experimental methods to the evaluation of practice and service. There is an increasing emphasis on accountability in all social welfare services today, including the health service. Health professionals are now being asked to set standards and measure the effects of what they are doing. Cost-effectiveness does not, however, have to mean the sacrifice of quality of care. Evaluation research is well suited to this task, yielding useful data for practitioners and service planners. The methods have been developed since the Second World War, especially in the United States, in industry and human services where there is a need to justify costs for continued funding.

Evaluation methods adopt the classic experimental design because it promises a way of systematically assessing change in services. There are difficulties of applying experiments in natural settings, of course, with associated problems of validity. As it is applied research other methods are often used within a broad experimental framework. Thus, in Lathlean and Farrish's (1984) study of ward sisters, a survey was used for the evaluation. Even qualitative methods such as unstructured interviews and observations have been used to collect data in an experimental design. For example, in Smith and Cantley's (1985) study of a new day hospital for ESMI (elderly mentally infirm) patients they interviewed staff and patients to determine the criteria for the success of the service. Unstructured observation was used in a similar study in an ESMI ward in Blandford (Couchman and Bradshaw, 1987). The mix of social science research methods is easily justified by reference to the argument for triangulation, discussed in the last chapter as a means of strengthening the validity of results.

To define 'evaluation research' we must distinguish it from the everyday usage of the word 'evaluation'. Luker (1981) points out that in everyday nursing evaluation simply means judgement. Evaluation research demands more systematic or scientific collection of information about people, performance or products in order to improve effectiveness.

Evaluation is designed to answer the question 'How are we doing?' and 'Are we achieving our goals?' – the effect of a new policy on nurse performance, for example. Weiss (1972) called it a comparison of 'What is' with 'What should be'. It follows a process of

Planning——→Action——→Evaluation

which corresponds to the problem-solving models we mentioned in the introductory chapters and to the experimental format:

1. A problem is stated.
2. An hypothesis is formulated for testing (i.e. a possible explanation is suggested).
3. Facts are gathered from observation or experimentation.
4. These facts are interpreted to see if the hypothesis was right.
5. Conclusions are drawn about solutions to the problem.

Evaluation, like experimental research, is concerned with before-and-after measures, comparing groups, the relationship between variables and controls. Our earlier example of the comparison of a community hospital and traditional hospital illustrates the approach well.

The terms 'evaluation research' and 'action research' are often used interchangeably, but evaluation research is more the measurement of past change, whereas action research incorporates the change or intervention into the study. The researcher, in fact, becomes the agent of change. It is more the comparison of 'What is' with 'What could be'. The process of Planning → Action → Evaluation is perhaps better viewed as a cycle where the evaluation stage, in turn, generates ideas for further planning and action. With more detail of the tasks and skills involved this would look like Figure 6.5.

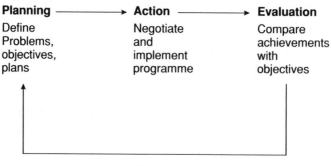

Feedback
close gap between
objectives and achievements

Figure 6.5 The evaluation cycle

Santayana, a philosopher, said:

> Those who cannot remember the past are condemned to repeat it.
> *Life of Reason* vol. I, ch. xii, 1905–6.

The difficulty in an evaluation study is finding the right indicators to measure, as in any quantitative study. Patton, who has written several imaginative books about evaluation says:

> 'Few things evade our attention so consistently as those things we take for granted.' (Patton, 1981)

Perhaps, then, in evaluating services or practice we are helping people to recognise what they already know but which they are not conscious. Luker (1981) has likened evaluation research to

Structure⟶Process⟶Outcome

in systems theory. This helps to highlight the fact that, although outcomes are important, we might need to take account of other variables – the 'means' as well as the 'ends'. The kind of factors you might consider in a nursing study could be:

1. *Structure:* facilities, equipment, staffing, style of management.
2. *Process:* forms of care.
3. *Outcome:* whether patients' objectives had been met.

Again, as Luker points out, this model coincides with the nursing process. The actual choice of variables would depend on the circumstances and purposes of the study.

Greenwood (1984) has suggested that action research is the only relevant research method for a practical discipline such as nursing. We would remind you, however, of the argument in Chapter 5. There is a danger in this kind of research, where the problems are defined by policy makers within unquestioned frameworks of knowledge. Smith and Cantley (1985) believe that researchers do not have to solve problems in the way they are expected to if they can demonstrate convincingly that the problem is best formulated another way. Perhaps the theory and values bases need to be made explicit at the outset. It is useful to identify sometimes whether the research is intended to meet the needs of the clients or the service, because the ideas of the researcher and those who commissioned the research can be at odds.

If nurses are to become involved in evaluation, they must enter into a dialogue as professionals developing their own theories and values of care. Evaluation can be 'formative' (Morris and Fitz-Gibbon, 1978; Burton, 1986) so that the researchers play an interactive role in the collection and sharing of information with practitioners and planners during the development of a programme of care.

This particular approach can be helpful in overcoming any resistance from practitioners in the work setting. The idea of an outsider coming in to evaluate can be extremely threatening. If people are involved in the research they are more likely to use the results.

Patton (1982) calls it a 'Collaborative Evaluation' model. It is a team effort with team members representing different groups or disciplines who have a stake in the outcome (Patton describes them as 'stake-holders'). This model was used in the Blandford study quoted earlier (Couchman and Bradshaw, 1987) and in other studies in the mental health field (Towell and Harries, 1979; Evans and Blunden, 1984).

The last words should go to Patton (1981) who reminds us not to take evaluation too seriously:

> Him to her
> Evaluators make better lovers because they are constantly assessing their performance to improve it.
>
> Her to him
> Being aware of a thing and being able to do something about it are two quite different things!

Exercises

Here are some light-hearted exercises on experiments and evaluation that you might like to try out, either on your own or with a group of colleagues.

1. Advertisers are always telling us that Soap Powder X washes more clothes than Powder Y, or one brand of washing-up liquid washes more than another. Design an experiment to see if one brand of washing-up liquid really does wash more dishes than another. We have provided some questions to prompt you in your design.

Question
How would you word the hypothesis?

Which is the independent and which the dependent variable?

How could the dependent variable be measured?

What factors could act as confounding variables, and how could you control for these?

Answers
The hypothesis would probably be something like:

> Liquid detergent A will wash more dishes than liquid detergent B.

The *null* hypothesis would be

There will be no difference in the number of dishes washed by liquid detergent A compared with liquid detergent B.

The independent variables are the washing-up liquids, whereas the number of dishes washed is the dependent variable.

One way of comparing the liquids that you have probably thought of is to see how many dishes one measure of liquid A can wash in one session compared with an equivalent measure of liquid B. The confounding variables would be that:

- The same person did both sets of washing-up. The water was the same temperature.
- Both sets of dishes were equally greasy.
- The detergent was added to the water at the same point.
- The agitation of the detergent in the water should be the same.
- The point at which you judge how many dishes have been washed must be fixed: is it when there are no more bubbles in the water or when the dishes no longer look clean (and what is the criterion for 'clean')?

You may think of other considerations: differences in skin temperature or cleanliness, for instance, or the order in which you tried the different detergents. One way around this in an experimental design would be to conduct more than one trial, with the order in which you used the detergents being decided randomly by the toss of a coin.

2. Staff Nurse Baker has decided to compare the ease of reference of new nursing process notes on one half of her ward with the old ones on the other half. Try answering the following questions to help you in designing the study:

- Is this a classic experimental design?
- What other methods could be used?
- How should the subjects be chosen?
- How many are needed?
- What would be the hypothesis?
- What are the independent and dependent variables?
- What measures could be used?
- Could they be valid and reliable?
- What are the possible confounding variables to control for?
- Can you satisfy the rules of causality?
- Can you generalise the results to other groups?
- Is the design ethically sound?

Discussion
The first task is to decide how to measure 'ease of reference'. You could observe how frequently staff actually referred to the notes, but that could

be very time-consuming for a 'part-time' researcher, even if you only observe for sample times of the day. You could focus the observation to the number of times notes were referred to during ward rounds, but there is still a considerable time commitment. You could conduct a survey or interview with staff for their opinions on the new notes, but that could be rather subjective.

One way would be to use measures from the nursing process notes themselves, such as how many goals were set and achieved for patients and changes made to the notes on the basis of evaluation. These are reasonably valid indicators, according to the various criteria. The hypothesis for the study would then be:

'The new nursing process notes will make it easier for nurses to keep notes up to date'.

The independent variable is the introduction of the new system for notes and the dependent variable the frequency of additions to the notes.

3. Imagine that I have to buy a house for you. List the factors that you would want me to remember when selecting a suitable house. Now ask other people you know to make such a list and compare the two.

Discussion

The important point here is that whereas the two lists would have some common factors, there would also be many more differences. Different people have different perspectives on what would be a successful outcome and the same applies to evaluation research.

Smith and Cantley (1985) studied an ESMI day hospital using a 'pluralistic' evaluation to represent the views of the different groups involved (and to triangulate results). In interviews with staff and families they revealed quite contradictory criteria for the success of the service. The staff perceived the carers' support group as providing relief to families and preventing admission to long-term care, so assumed that the service should be evaluated in those terms. The majority of carers, on the other hand, when interviewed said that they only attended the support group in an attempt to persuade the staff to admit their relative to care!

REFERENCES

Boore J (1978) *A Prescription for Recovery.* London: Royal College of Nursing.
Burton M (1986) What do we mean by Evaluation? *Health Service Journal,* **17** July: 954–955.
Cook T D and Campbell D T (1979) *Quasi-experimentation: Design and Analysis Issues for Field Studies.* Chicago: Rand McNally.
Couchman W and Bradshaw P (1987) A Measure of the lifestyles of two groups

of elderly mentally ill people. Paper presented at 'In Pursuit of Excellence' Conference, London, 2 November 1987.

Evans G and Blunden R (1984) A collaborative approach to evaluation. *Journal of Practical Approaches to Developmental Handicap*, **8** (1): 14–18.

Greenwood J (1984) Nursing Research: a position paper. *Journal of Advanced Nursing*, **9** (1); 77–82.

Hayward J (1975) *Information: a Prescription Against Pain*. London: Royal College of Nursing.

Lathlean J and Farrish S (1984) *The Ward Sister Training Project: An Evaluation of a Training Scheme for Ward Sisters*. London: DHSS.

Lorenson M (1983) Effects of touch in patients during a crisis situation in hospital. In: Wilson-Barnett J (ed), *Nursing Research: Ten Studies in Patient Care*, ch 9. Chichester: Wiley.

Luker K (1981) An overview of evaluation research in nursing. *Journal of Advanced Nursing*, **6**: 87–93.

Miller P McC and Wilson M J (1983) *A Dictionary of Social Science Methods*. Chichester: Wiley.

Morris L L and Fitz-Gibbon C T (1978) *Program Evaluation Kit*. London: Sage.

Open University (1984) *Research Methods in Education and the Social Sciences*. Milton Keynes: Open University Press.

Patton M Q (1981) *Creative Evaluation*. London: Sage.

Patton M Q (1982) *Practical Evaluation*. London: Sage.

Robson C (1983) *Experiment, Design and Statistics in Psychology*, 2nd edn, Harmondsworth: Penguin Books.

Smith G and Cantley C (1985) Policy evaluation: the use of varied data in a study of a psychogeriatric service. In: Walter R (ed), *Applied Qualitative Research*, pp. 156–174. London: Gower.

Towell D and Harries C (1979) *Innovation in Patient Care*. London: Croom Helm.

Weiss C H (1972) *Evaluation Research: Methods for Assessing Program Effectiveness*. Englewood Cliffs, NJ: Prentice Hall.

FURTHER READING

Cormack D F S (ed.) (1984) *The Research Process in Nursing*, chs 10 and 13. Oxford: Blackwell.

Miller S (1975) *Experimental Design and Statistics*. London: Methuen.

Polit D and Hungler B (1983) *Nursing Research: Principles and Methods*, ch. 6. Philadelphia: J B Lippincott.

Treece E W and Treece J W (1977) *Elements of Research in Nursing*. New York: Mosby.

7

Surveys

The survey is probably the research method that we are all most familiar with. Almost all of us at some time will have been stopped in the street for a market research survey of our opinions of some biscuits or domestic cleaner or other product. There is also the census, of course, which is a survey on a massive scale involving everyone in the country. You may also have taken part in a survey at work by completing a questionnaire on, for instance, back pain or testing a new product or procedure.

Because it is such a familiar method many people who want to do a research project feel that they must do a survey when, as we pointed out in Chapter 5 on research design, there is a range of methods to choose from. It is important to start with your research question and then find the best method to address it, rather than finding a question to fit the method.

Familiarity with the method can also breed contempt. Some people seem to believe that, like writing a novel, designing a questionnaire is something that anyone can do without any kind of training. This shows, unfortunately, in quite a lot of questionnaires that are used in research and the researcher is doomed to learn from his or her mistakes. Questions are asked in ways that will produce invalid or meaningless responses. A few simple guidelines can help to avoid wasted time and effort.

DEFINITION

A survey, as we defined it in Chapter 5, is:

> The use of questionnaires, tests and interviews with large samples of the population.

Like the experimental methods discussed in the last chapter, the survey usually starts with some form of hypothesis and is concerned with quantifying variables and their relationships. The principle is that if you administer the same stimulus in the form of uniform questions you can compare the variation in the responses. As the method derives from the social sciences, however, it is not perhaps aiming for the same level of scientific rigour and control as an experiment.

SURVEY STYLES

There are two basic means of data collection in surveys: the postal or self-completion questionnaire and the interview, although the same rules of design generally apply to both. Which type you choose will depend on certain constraints such as cost.

The *self-completion* type is relatively cheap, even if postage is involved. Instructions for completion must, however, be very clear and precise.

Interviews can be very time consuming and interviewers may need to be paid. There are problems about consistency of style if more than one interviewer is used. Characteristics of the interviewer may influence the respondents, if they are of a different age, gender or class. On the other hand, face-to-face interaction can be a great advantage, because the interviewer has the opportunity to probe certain areas in more depth. Just as there is a continuum of research methods from the most to the least structured, so survey styles vary by degree of structure. At one end of the scale is the large survey with a structured questionnaire or interview schedule. At the other end of the scale is the unstructured interview. In between are various semi-structured formats for questionnaires and interviews. 'Structure' refers to whether the questions themselves are open or closed. To illustrate the differences between structured, semi-structured and unstructured formats we are including some short and simple examples in Figures 7.1, 7.2 and 7.3.

The exact choice of style depends very much on the purpose of the research. If the research is fairly exploratory, where you are trying to find out something about a little-known area, then a structured questionnaire with closed questions such as Figure 7.1 would not really be appropriate. It would impose your assumptions through the choice of questions and answers. You will only get what you are looking for, not what others want to say. You are setting your boundaries on the area of interest when what we really want to know here is what the people in that area think are the boundaries. The best style in this case would be a fairly open and qualitative interview to allow you to explore freely (as in Figures 7.2 and 7.3).

Obviously, this approach is quite time consuming and is best suited to numbers less than 50 who are reasonably representative of the group under study. We will be discussing the approach in more detail in Chapter 8, on qualitative techniques.

Qualitative methods are beginning to be used more in nursing research where in-depth investigation of a variety of settings is needed. Some of these studies are reported in Wilson-Barnett (1983).

WHERE ARE YOU NOW?

If you are a part-time nursing degree graduate we would be grateful if you could answer the following questions:

1. In which area was you career *before* the degree?
   (Please tick one box)
   Clinical/Community ☐
   Education ☐
   Management ☐
   Other ☐
   (If 'Other' please specify)

   ....

2. In which area was you career *during* the degree?
   (Please tick one box)
   Clinical/Community ☐
   Education ☐
   Management ☐
   Other ☐
   (if 'Other' please specify)

   ....

3. In which area was you career *after* the degree?
   (Please tick one box)
   Clinical/Community ☐
   Education ☐
   Management ☐
   Other ☐
   (if 'Other' please specify)

   ....

4. Are you . . .
   (Tick one box)
   Female? ☐
   Male? ☐

5. Do you have any other comments?
   (Please write overleaf)

MANY THANKS FOR YOUR HELP

Figure 7.1 An example of a structured questionnaire

READING HABITS SURVEY

1. Which nursing journals do you read?

2. Do you buy any nursing journals?
   (if YES, which ones?)

3. When do you read journals (at work, at home, etc.)?

4. Which topics do you like to read about?

5. How far away is your nearest hospital library?

6. When did you last visit a hospital library?

Thanks for your help

Figure 7.2 An example of a structured interview schedule

Structured questionnaires like Figure 7.1 are the ideal method for obtaining information from large numbers of people. They can be used to gain data on attitudes, beliefs and opinions from a wide range of people relatively quickly and cheaply. The data lends itself to statistical analysis to show large-scale social patterns and trends. It follows that the style is best used for numbers of approximately 100 and above, and in an area where the boundaries for research are already quite well established.

Many nursing studies have taken this approach successfully. Structured

---

VIEWS ON NURSING PROCESS – INTERVIEW GUIDE

(Ask the questions in your own words, and in a different order if appropriate.
Probe as necessary.)

Introduction
Introduce self as student doing course.
Explain that doing study as project on views of qualified nurses about the
nursing process.
Stress confidentiality.

Main questions
1. Does the nurse use the nursing process?
2. If used, how is it used?
3. Definition of nursing process?
4. How learned/trained about nursing process?
5. Level of commitment to nursing process?
6. Statement of pros and cons?

Background details
Age
Speciality
Year qualified
Postbasic qualifications

(Thank interviewee.)

Figure 7.3 An example of a semi-structured interview guide

surveys have been used to assess nurses' attitudes towards their role, their
practice, their training and towards specific groups of patients. Patients
have been asked for their opinions on their care before admission, and
before and after leaving hospital. Macleod Clark and Hockey (1979, 1988)
provide a useful summary of many of these studies.

On the other side of the coin, the disadvantages of the structured method
are that it can be a little too broad, general and superficial. There is also
the vexed question of validity. How can you be sure that your questions
mean the same to everyone and will elicit accurate information on the
subject you are interested in? Sometimes it feels as if the respondents are
being pigeon-holed, or forced into artificial categories.

The other major problem is the 'words/deeds dilemma' – people will say one thing and do another. For example, a respondent might be able to tell you all about the importance of exercise for health, and in reality lead a very sedentary life. Most of the guidelines on the design of questionnaires exist to try and tackle this problem, and we have given some useful references at the end of this chapter.

PROCEDURE

There are three main stages in constructing a structured questionnaire for a survey:

1. Exploratory stage.
2. Pilot study.
3. Main survey.

Stages 1 and 2 are very important to overcome some of the problems in the main survey that we have discussed.

Exploratory stage

This stage is very much like the unstructured or qualitative interviews we mentioned earlier and like the example in Figure 7.3. The idea is that you spend some time in the setting you want to study, observing and talking to several people fairly informally to establish the boundaries and see what the main issues are. Your informal chats would be focused by the hypotheses of the study. Working from the notes you make, you are more likely to design a structured questionnaire later on that asks relevant questions. It is usually a mistake to assume that, without exploratory work, you already know what questions to ask in a survey. You may be biased by your own views.

Pilot study

On the basis of your exploratory work you should now be in a position to draft some semi-structured questions. This means asking questions on the issues raised in the exploratory stage in a way that will elicit the range of answers you are likely to encounter. At this stage it is probably better to leave the questions fairly open-ended or allow room for comments, so that people may talk freely on the topics. See Figure 7.2 as an example. In order to assess the range of issues and possible responses it is a good idea to include between 20 and 50 people in your pilot study, depending on the breadth and depth of topics to be studied.

Main survey

The results of your pilot study should give you enough information to design a structured questionnaire, i.e. closed questions with fixed choice responses such as those shown in Figure 7.1. The structuring of questions is covered in a later section.

In a very large survey there might be further drafts of the questionnaire or schedule for checking and refining. Even with thorough preparation at the exploratory and pilot stages, it is inevitable that you will get the wording of some questions wrong.

If you decide to go ahead on the first draft of the main survey it is still worth a 'suck it and see' test. Try the questionnaire out on a few people to see if they understand all the questions and how to answer them.

It is at this point that decisions about design, question wording and structuring of answers need to be finalised. The size of sample must be decided. Someone with statistical expertise should also be consulted. You might want to consider computer analysis of your results. All of these matters will be dealt with in the rest of the chapter.

DESIGN

There are five main rules about questionnaire design:

1. Ask questions that are easy to understand and answer.
2. Give clear instructions.
3. Adopt a format that eases analysis.
4. Allow questions to flow to maintain interest.
5. Consider overall impressions.

Ask questions that are easy to understand and answer

Don't over-estimate the ability of the respondent. It has been said that the average reading age of the population is 9 years, and that *The Sun* newspaper is written with that in mind. Too many questionnaires are written in the language of the middle-class professional. Questions should be short and simple.

Give clear instructions

Spell out exactly how the respondent should answer the questions, even if the survey is conducted by interview. State, for example, whether more than one answer is possible to a multiple-choice question, whether boxes are to be ticked, numbers circled, etc. Figure 7.1 gives some examples where one box is to be ticked, because only one answer is thought to be possible. An example of a multiple-choice question is shown in Figure 7.4.

---

1. How do you get information   Nursing press   ☐
    on post-registration courses?   Management   ☐
    (Please tick more than one   School of Nursing   ☐
    answer if appropriate)   Colleagues   ☐
                                        Other   ☐

If 'Other' please specify ....

Figure 7.4 An example of a multiple-choice question

Notice that space is given for comments even in a structured questionnaire, so that people can still have some freedom of response. Make it clear what people should do if they answer 'no' to a question – should they move on to a later question? See the example in Figure 7.5.

---

1. Have you changed jobs since obtaining the degree
    (Please tick one box)   Yes   ☐
                                                  No   ☐

If 'Yes' please answer Question 2.
If 'No' please go to Question 3.

Figure 7.5 An example of a question with instructions for respondents

Another method is to treat the questions like a flow chart and draw arrows to the next appropriate question. You may have noticed that this method is now being used to simplify official forms (See Figure 7.6). Questionnaires of this type need careful editing because respondents can get hopelessly lost among the different options.

Adopt a format that eases analysis

It will be easier and quicker at the analysis stage if all the answers are ranged down the right-hand side of the page as in our examples. Some questionnaires leave an additional column for coding on the right edge of the page, marked 'Office use only' (Figure 7.1), or 'Please leave blank' or 'Do not write in this column'. We will be dealing with the question of coding later.

Allow questions to flow to maintain interest

Questions should be logically ordered and interesting. The opening questions should grab the respondent's interest which is why it is not

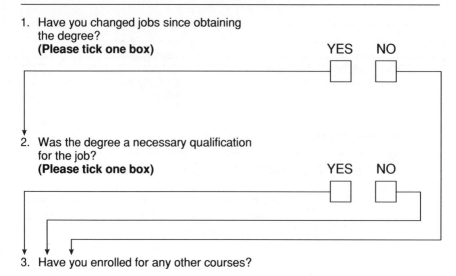

Figure 7.6 An example of branching questions

always sensible to start with personal details such as age, occupation, salary, etc., especially if these include sensitive areas. They may be best left to the end, so that you launch straight into the important topics but at a light, non-threatening level at first. Then you can move on to the more weighty matters of interest. The flow of questions can be represented as:

Easy⸺→Meat⸺→Personal details

In a survey of nurses' views on financial constraints in the NHS, for instance, it would make sense to start the questionnaire with some routine details of how the individual is affected by cuts in their daily work, before seeking more political views.

Consider overall impressions

Pay attention to the look of the questionnaire. Is the layout attractive and pleasant to use? What about the length? It should be as short as possible, otherwise the respondent may become tired and bored or not even bother at all. Remember your own experiences with questionnaires.

Be ruthless about which questions to include. Resist the temptation to ask everything connected with the topic that might be interesting, and 'weed out' questions in the final stages. Remember also the amount of data you are generating. If you ask 100 people 20 questions then you will have 2000 items of data to handle!

Give some introduction to the questionnaire and the topic. You may

PROFESSIONAL DEVELOPMENT SURVEY

I am a student undertaking a project as part of a course in nursing research methods, and I am interested in the views of qualified nurses in Southshire on the current debate about professional development. I would, therefore, be most grateful if you could complete this short questionnaire and return it as soon as possible to me in the enclosed stamped, addressed envelope. Any details that you give will be anonymous and confidential. I hope to publish the results later in the nursing press. Please let me know if you would like any further details.

Figure 7.7 An example of an introductory paragraph for a questionnaire

include this as an introductory paragraph on the questionnaire itself (Figure 7.7) or include a covering letter (Figure 7.8).

In either case you need to interest the reader in the topic, stressing its relevance or importance, in order to gain their co-operation. Explain, therefore, why you are doing a survey, what it is for and how you are doing it.

Always maintain a polite tone – for example 'Please tick one answer'. Thank the respondent heartily both before doing the questionnaire (in the introduction or letter) and afterwards – for example, 'Thank you so much for your help'. You might also want to offer details of the results if people are interested – for example, 'Please tick this box if you would be interested in receiving details of the results of the survey'.

Do not forget to stress confidentiality and anonymity, as our examples show, if that is what you are offering.

QUESTION WORDING

Remember that people do not always behave in the way they say they do. People generally like to please, so they may try very hard to give you the answer they think you want. The trick is to ask questions in such a way that you get as close as possible to the truth.

Here are some *do's* and *don'ts* on the wording of questions in questionnaires.

Don't use long complex questions.
Do keep questions clear and simple.

For example:

'Do you think student nurses should get more pay?'

is more straightforward than:

Dept of Nursing,
Hightown College,
Southshire

(date)

Dear Colleague,

We are a group of students undertaking a project as part of a course in nursing research methods.

We would like to find out what contribution a part-time nursing degree makes towards professional development. To discover this, we thought it appropriate to canvass a sample of degree graduates throughout the country to find out their career patterns.

A questionnaire is enclosed. When completed, we would be grateful if it could be returned to us in the stamped, addressed envelope. Any details that you give will be anonymous and confidential.

Results of the survey will be published at a later date in the nursing press, or a report will be available from us if required.

Thank you for your help.

Yours faithfully,

Course Representative

Figure 7.8 An example of a covering letter for a questionnaire

'There's been a lot of talk in the media about pay awards for different grades, especially student nurses. What do you think?'

Don't ask double-barrelled questions.
Do ask one question at a time.

'Are you satisfied with the pay offer or do you think there should be further negotiations?'

is actually two questions in one. If someone answers 'Yes', which question are they answering? It needs to be translated into two or more questions.

Don't ask leading questions.
Do word questions neutrally.

A leading question runs along the lines of:

'Do you agree that . . .?', 'Don't you think it would be a good idea if . . .?' or 'would it be better if . . .'

It leads the respondent to the answer suggested by the question, rather than their own view. An example would be:

'Do you believe that it is unethical for nurses to strike?'

A more neutral approach is to simply invite respondents to state their opinions:

'Please state your views on whether nurses should strike',

or provide a range of views as a multiple-choice question.

Don't ask hypothetical questions.
Do make questions concrete and individual.

'If you were the prime minister what would you do about the NHS?'

is too hypothetical and will not provide very useful information.

'Do you have any suggestions for cost-effective changes in your ward?'

might be more realistic.

Don't ask embarrassing questions.
Do be indirect in sensitive areas.

Direct questions about pay, politics and controversial topics such as abortion are likely to produce guarded responses. It is such better to present a range of statements to which people can state their agreement or disagreement.

Don't use vague, ambiguous words.
Do be specific.

'How far do you walk each day?'

is preferable to:

'How much exercise do you get?'

Don't use jargon or highbrow words.
Do use simple language.

People will understand:

'Do you take aspirin or paracetamol when the pain starts?'

better than:

'Do you need analgesics?'

Don't ask recall questions.

Do give memory guides.

If you ask questions such as:

'How often do you go to the doctor's?'

you will get inaccurate responses. Guides such as:

'How many times have you been to the doctor's in the last week/month/6 months, etc.?'

are more reliable.

Don't ask proxy questions.
Do question people direct.

Never ask a wife, for instance, about her husband's health. Ask him directly.

WAYS OF STRUCTURING ANSWERS

When you are structuring answers on a questionnaire there are alternative types to choose from:

- Open questions
- Yes/No
- Multiple-choice, cafeteria or checklist
- Rank ordering
- Graded alternatives
- Combination of checklist and grading
- Attitude scales

Open questions

We have already referred to open and semi-structured questions and given examples in Figures 7.2 and 7.3.

Yes/no or fixed choice questions

Examples of this type can be found in Figures 7.1 and 7.5.

Multiple-choice, cafeteria or check-list

This is the type of question we discussed earlier, where one or more answer is possible. An example is given in Figure 7.9.

What does the word 'healthy' mean to you?
(Please tick one or more answers)

a)	Living to be very old	☐
b)	Never having a cold	☐
c)	Hardly ever going to the doctor	☐
d)	Eating the right foods	☐
e)	Exercising regularly	☐
f)	Feeling happy and well	☐
g)	Being able to look after yourself	☐
h)	Other (please specify below)	☐

Figure 7.9 A multiple-choice, cafeteria or check-list question

Rank ordering

The rank order question invites respondents to put a list of items in order of preference or, in other words, to grade or score them. For example, see Figure 7.10. A variation on this approach in an interview is to provide the respondent with cards, one for each category, to sort into order of importance.

Please indicate the order of importance to you of these things in life.
Place a 1 beside the most important, 2 beside the next most important, and so on:

a)	Achievement at work	——
b)	Family relationships	——
c)	Friendships/social life	——
d)	Health	——
e)	Money	——
f)	Religion	——
g)	Other (please specify below)	——

Figure 7.10 An example of a rank-ordering question

1. Are you encouraged to apply for study days?
   (Please tick one box)

Always	☐
Sometimes	☐
Never	☐

2. In general, how healthy do you consider yourself?
   (Please tick one box)

Very healthy	☐
Fairly healthy	☐
Fairly unhealthy	☐
Very unhealthy	☐

Figure 7.11 Examples of graded alternatives questions

Graded alternatives

Some examples of this are shown in Figure 7.11.

Combination of checklist and grading

The example for this is shown in Figure 7.12. In the example some questions are stated as negatives so that respondents have to consider each one. The tendency when all statements are positive is to tick automatically down the 'agree' columns.

Please tick one box for each of the following statements:

Professional development . . .	Strongly agree	Agree	Disagree	Strongly disagree
a) Keeps you up to date	☐	☐	☐	☐
b) Is not for promotion	☐	☐	☐	☐
c) Is not directly relevant to patient care	☐	☐	☐	☐
d) Helps with teaching students	☐	☐	☐	☐

Figure 7.12 An example of a combined check-list and grading question

Attitude scales

The best known of this type are the Thurstone, Likert and Guttman scales and the Semantic Differential technique. They are similar to the graded alternative question type, but more technical. They need to be carefully constructed and tested to be statistically viable. If you are seriously considering this kind of question we suggest that you refer to one of the guides to survey methods, such as Moser and Kalton (1971), quoted at the end of the chapter. The Repertory Grid is another method along similar lines that you may encounter and want to find out more about (Oppenheim, 1966). On the whole it is best to aim for a balance of answer types including one or two open questions. This gives respondents an interesting variety – it can be very boring to answer a whole series of yes/no or multiple-choice questions. Open questions allow the respondents space for comments and expression of their feelings. In an interview the interviewer can probe and prompt on open questions. The resulting qualitative data is usually very rich, and lends support and substance to quantitative results.

With closed questions the general rule is that categories should be mutually exclusive, exhaustive and not overlapping. A common mistake is to overlap categories such as age bands, as shown in Figure 7.13.

What is your age? **(Tick one box)**	Under 20	☐
	20–25	☐
	25–30	☐
	Over 30	☐

Figure 7.13 An example of a question with overlapping categories – 1

With this banding a person of 20, 25 or 30 years could actually tick two boxes. Similar problems arise over definitions of terms, such as the case in Figure 7.14 where divorced, separated and widowed people would also be single status, and could be a single parent as well, so that an individual might tick three boxes!

What is your marital status? **(Tick one box)**	Married	☐
	Single	☐
	Divorced	☐
	Separated	☐
	Widowed	☐
	Single parent	☐

Figure 7.14 An example of a question with overlapping categories – 2

SURVEY OF PATIENTS' VISITORS

1. How old are you?   —

2. What is the patient in hospital for?   Minor surgery   ☐
                                          Major surgery   ☐

3. Are you the patient's . . .   Spouse?   ☐
                                          Son/daughter?   ☐
                                          Brother/sister?   ☐

4. Do you think visiting time is organised   Yes   ☐
    properly?   No   ☐

5. How do you travel to the hospital?   Walk   ☐
                                          Public transport   ☐
                                          By car   ☐

6. Do you agree that sister should speak   Yes   ☐
    to all visitors?   No   ☐

7. Are you married with children?
    (Please state how many)   —

8. Which social class do you belong to?:   Working class   ☐
                                          Middle class   ☐
                                          Upper class   ☐

Figure 7.15 An example of a 'bad' questionnaire for exercise

Worked example

Test your understanding of the rules of question wording and structure by criticising the 'bad' questionnaire in Figure 7.15. How many deliberate mistakes can you find? A good test of any questionnaire which you might like to try is to answer the questions yourself, seeing how far you can misinterpret them.

Discussion
   Question 1
   A startling start to the questionnaire. This type of question is best asked at the end, and in a more indirect way – i.e. 'Which of these age bands applies to you?'

Question 2
Not only is the question asking for information by proxy, it is assuming that the respondent has knowledge of hospital jargon such as 'minor' and 'major' surgery.

Question 3
There are no answer categories other than close relatives, and no space for others to be added.

Question 4
A vague, unspecified question that is difficult to answer, especially with a 'Yes' or 'No'. The question needs to be more specific and a range of answers offered, with instructions as to whether one or more answer is possible.

Question 5
The answer categories here overlap. They do not allow for the fact that someone might travel to the hospital by more than one of these methods – for example, part of the way by bus, part on foot.

Question 6
It sounds as if this is what the survey is all about, and the researcher wants to prove a point: a very leading question. Again, with a 'Yes/No' response, no room is left for degrees of opinion.

Question 7
This is a double- (or even triple-) barrelled question. With the lack of guidelines, erratic responses are likely.

Question 8
What an embarrassing question! What would your response be? If social class is an important variable, it is better to ask for occupation and work out the class by the Registrar General's classification later.

You may have found many other points to criticise. It really is a bad questionnaire, but questions similar to these appear regularly in surveys.

SAMPLING

It is at the design stage that you need to prepare a sample group, although broad decisions about sampling may already have been made at an earlier stage. Most surveys are based on a sample because, with the exception of the census, there is not enough time or resources to acquire information on the total group of interest.

Definitions

Sampling is the process of selecting a portion of the population to represent the entire population. A sample therefore is a subset of a population selected to participate in a research study. A population is the aggregate of all cases of interest with common characteristic(s).

If you wanted to do a survey on drinking and driving, then you would draw your sample from the national population over the age of 16 years, whereas the population for a survey of nurses might be restricted to qualified nurses in a certain geographical area only.

A major consideration, therefore, is the degree to which the sample represents the population. In particular you need to beware of bias – the under- or over-representation of certain groups. Otherwise you may have to qualify your findings.

In the example of the drinking and driving survey, if our sample contained more women than men and more than half were under 30 years then we could only report findings that applied to those groups. We could not claim that they were representative of the adult population as a whole.

Rules

There are certain rules to follow in sampling so that you can be more confident about generalising the results of your sample to the rest of the population.

It is generally better if the sampling is based on probability methods, although these are often seen as more costly because they take longer. Probability methods mean that the sample is randomly selected from the population, rather like selecting names from a hat. The four most common methods of sampling are:

- Simple sampling
- Stratified sampling
- Cluster sampling
- Quota sampling

Worked example

In order to illustrate the principles of sampling, imagine that you have to arrange an exchange visit for a British hospital of 500 staff with a French hospital, but there is only one coach with 50 places available. What would be the fairest way of sharing out the places?

Simple sampling
This is where you choose randomly from the total population. You could simply put the 500 staff names in a hat and take 50 out, like a raffle or a lottery. This can be somewhat time consuming and so a more straightforward method is to choose 50 names from a list of all the names, either using a random number table to decide the order of choice, or by taking every tenth name (calculated from the fraction of 500 divided by 50), perhaps starting with a randomly chosen number.

Stratified sampling

You might decide that certain groups needed to be represented on the visit – doctors, nurses, therapists, for instance. Simple random sampling might leave some of them out.

Stratified sampling allows for chosen groups to be in a sample by randomly selecting within strata. To choose the sample therefore we must first decide on the groups or strata (doctors, nurses, therapists, etc.) and then make a simple random choice within each group. If, for instance, we had five groups to be represented we could choose 10 from each group, although the number might depend on the size of each group. If there were twice as many nurses as doctors, for instance, we might choose 13 nurses and seven doctors – unless you considered that doctors were more important and needed more representatives!

Cluster sampling

Let us extend this example a little and imagine that the group from our hospital is one of several going from all over Britain. The selection of groups could have been achieved by cluster sampling, which is a two-stage process of randomly chosen clusters. For example, some national organisation could have been invited by French authorities to arrange for 10 groups to visit. To be as fair as possible the organisers could have chosen 10 hospitals in simple random fashion from all British hospitals, and then instructed each hospital to make a random choice of 50 as we discussed above.

Quota sampling

This kind of sampling is not based on random methods but on the principle of fulfilling certain quotas. It has been developed mainly in the field of market research. You may have had the experience of being approached in the street by a market researcher saying, 'I've been looking for a woman of your age'!

To return to our example, we could have decided in advance how many of each profession we wanted to be represented on the French visit, according to some criteria such as relevance or importance. If we decided on 10 of each of five groups – doctors, nurses, therapists, administrators, health authority members – we could then go to each group and ask for 10 people to be nominated to fill our quota for that group.

In most surveys a stratified sample is best because it helps to ensure that the sample is representative on key variables, for example specialty or qualification. The quota method is not so favoured because of the possibility of bias, but it is quicker and cheaper than random choice methods. There are times when one may have to compromise because there isn't the freedom to choose a random sample. If, for example, you wanted to survey the views of nurses locally on a particular topic but couldn't get access to computerised staff records to work out a random sample, you might estimate a quota sample and approach colleagues with a reasonable balance of age and experience.

Size of sample

There is no hard and fast rule about sample size. A rough rule of thumb is to use as large a sample as possible. Aim for more than 100 if you want to include different groups and do quite a lot of statistics with your data: 200–300 is a respectable number if you are doing a serious survey. Any more might become unmanageable.

The size of sample will, of course, depend on the size of the total population and the variety of groups within it that need to be represented. With certain groups it might be feasible to use the whole population – for example, all trained nurses in a hospital or district.

INTERVIEW SKILLS

If you are doing your survey via interviews, the necessary social skills would have to be taken into account. Interviews are discussed again in more detail in the chapter on qualitative methods but we would like to stress here the importance of attending to skills, because the interview has to be handled properly as a brief social interaction between strangers. We mentioned earlier the importance of consistency in approach between interviewers. In large surveys interviewers are trained before the survey starts and the matching between interviewer and respondent is carefully considered.

RESPONSE RATES

Rate of response can be a problem, especially with postal and self-completion questionnaires. The number of questionnaires returned can obviously vary between 0% and 100%.

As discussed earlier, it is important that the sample is representative of the population and if a large proportion of the sample do not respond the sample may become biased. Non-responders can differ from responders on key characteristics which influence their ability or time to respond. Men tend to be worse responders than women. The elderly, the rurally based and lower socioeconomic groups are less likely to respond.

The accepted 'cut-off' rate for response to surveys is 65%, although the higher the better. Some quite respectable surveys, however, have reported results from lower response rates.

Strategies

Different strategies have been suggested to overcome the problems of non-response before and after the survey. More details of these can be found in the references at the end of the chapter.

Before

Careful pilot work and a well-designed questionnaire with a covering letter will go a long way to reducing non-response. A stamped addressed envelope can help, although this adds to the cost of the survey, of course. If you can engage people's interest they are more likely to respond. Sometimes incentives are used, such as copies of the results, or an invitation to a meeting. Market research firms often offer free gifts.

After

Reminders can be effective if firm and timed right. Hoinville and Jowell (1977) showed that responses can be boosted by 20% (from around 40% to 60%) after a first reminder 10 days after the initial mailing, and a further 10% (up to 70+ %) after a second reminder at around 20 days. Some researchers send another copy of the questionnaire with the second reminder.

Non-responders are sometimes followed up personally with an interview. This is not possible if the questionnaire was anonymous. The responses for follow-ups can be used as a sample of the non-responders and as a check on any bias in the group of responders. If necessary the results could be weighted to compensate for bias. In the case of non-response because people refuse, have moved on or are on holiday, you could select a substitute with matching characteristics.

CODING RESULTS

Results from questionnaires that are to be analysed statistically by computer need to be coded into number form ready for 'punching in' or processing by the computer programme. Figure 7.16 shows how responses to our earlier sample questionnaire in Figure 7.1 have been coded in the right-hand column.

Alternatively, the codes can be transferred to a 'coding sheet' which eases and speeds up the 'punching in' (see Figure 7.17). There is a box for each digit and space for the results from several questionnaires.

The conventions for converting results to codes are fairly straightforward. In simple 'Yes/No' categorisation, 'Yes' is coded as 1 and 'No' as 2. A list of items in a multiple-choice question is numbered from 1 onwards, as in our example in Figure 7.16. In a multiple-choice question which allows for more than one answer, however, each item on the list

WHERE ARE YOU NOW?   *Office use*

If you are a part-time nursing degree graduate we would be grateful if you could answer the following questions:

1. In which area was you career *before* the degree?
    (Please tick one box)
    Clinical/Community   ☑   1
    Education   ☐
    Management   ☐
    Other   ☐
    (If 'Other' please specify)

    ....

2. In which area was you career *during* the degree?
    (Please tick one box)
    Clinical/Community   ☐   2
    Education   ☑
    Management   ☐
    Other   ☐
    (if 'Other' please specify)

    ....

3. In which area was you career *after* the degree?
    (Please tick one box)
    Clinical/Community   ☐   2
    Education   ☑
    Management   ☐
    Other   ☐
    (if 'Other' please specify)

    ....

4. Are you . . .
    (Tick one box)
    Female?   ☑   1
    Male?   ☐

5. Do you have any other comments?
    (Please write overleaf)   2

MANY THANKS FOR YOUR HELP

Figure 7.16 An example of a coded questionnaire

'WHERE ARE YOU NOW?' SURVEY

ID			Q1	2	3	4	5
0	2	5	1	2	2	1	2

ID			Q1	2	3	4	5

ID			Q1	2	3	4	5

ID			Q1	2	3	4	5

ID			Q1	2	3	4	5

ID			Q1	2	3	4	5

ID			Q1	2	3	4	5

ID			Q1	2	3	4	5

ID			Q1	2	3	4	5

Figure 7.17 An example of a coding sheet

WHERE ARE YOU NOW? SURVEY

Coding Frame
ID   001–150
Q1.   1 = Clinical/Community
      2 = Education
      3 = Management
      4 = Other
Q2.   (as for Q1)
Q3.   (as for Q1)
Q4.   1 = Female
      2 = Male
Q5.   1 = Comments made
      2 = No comments

Figure 7.18 An example of a coding frame

needs to be treated as if it was a separate 'Yes/No' question and rated 1 or 2 according to whether it has a tick or not. To take the example given earlier under the heading 'Multiple-choice, cafeteria and checklist' respondents were invited to tick one or more answers from a list of statements about health. Each statement ticked would be coded 1 as if it was a separate question where the response was 'Yes'. Any statements not ticked would be coded 2, the equivalent of a 'No'. Missing data is conventionally coded 9.

To guide and interpret coding, you need to write a 'coding frame'. The coding frame for our example in Figures 7.16 and 7.17 would read something like Figure 7.18. You might find you want more guidelines on coding so some useful references are given at the end of the chapter (Hoinville and Jowell, 1977; Moser and Kalton, 1971; Oppenheim, 1966).

Any additional comments on a questionnaire, such as those made under 'Please specify' in our examples, can be analysed qualitatively (see Chapter 8 for discussion), or counted using a form of 'content analysis' (see Chapter 5) to be included on the coding sheet. This involves listing and tallying the most frequent responses to each question and combining them into categories so that the question can be treated as a multiple-choice type. The number of categories should ideally be less than 9, so that 9 can be used as the code for missing data. Figure 7.19 gives an example of the process for the open question 'Name one personal health issue that worries you', and Figure 7.20 the resulting codes.

Once the data has been processed it is ready for analysis by one of the many statistical packages available for small and large computers. We strongly recommend anyone who is interested in using computers to

Q1. Name one personal health issue that worries you

		TOTAL
Stroke	I	I
Infectious diseases	I	I
Rheumatism	II	2
Smoking	IIIII IIIII	10
Eczema	I	I
Heart disease	IIIII IIIII I	II
AIDS	IIIII IIIII IIIII IIIII IIII	24
Being overweight	IIIII I	6
Cancer	IIIII IIIII IIIII IIIII IIIII IIIII IIIII II	37
Arthritis	IIIII IIIII I	II
Diabetes	III	3
Kidneys	II	2
Stress	IIIII III	8
Alcohol	I	I
Not eating right food	II	2
Allergies	IIII	4
Asthma	II	3
Becoming disabled	II	2
Sinus	I	I
Blood pressure	I	I
Lack of exercise	I	I
Back problems	IIIII	5
Leukaemia	I	I
Breast cancer	I	I
Ageing	III	3
Overdoing exercise	I	I
Thyroid problems	I	I
Depression	I	I

Figure 7.19 An example of 'content analysis' of responses to open question

```
Coding frame

1 = Cancer
2 = AIDS
3 = Heart disease
4 = Smoking
5 = Stress
6 = Weight
7 = Arthritis
8 = Other
```

Figure 7.20 A coding frame for the open question in Figure 7.19

analyse their data to seek advice at an early stage on the design and coding of the questionnaire, and on the most suitable computer package for analysis. We will resume our discussion of data analysis in Chapter 9.

SURVEY EXERCISES

1. This exercise can be conducted individually or in a group. It is designed to help you develop a structured questionnaire or interview schedule through exploratory and pilot stages:
   (a) Explore a suitable topic for a survey through discussion and observation in the kind of setting you want to study.
   (b) Refine the topic area by defining specific hypotheses and key variables.
   (c) Choose the most important variables for the survey.
   (d) Draft some 'open-ended' questions on these variables.
   (e) Address these questions to a number of people and record their responses.
   (f) Decide how each question is best translated into a 'closed' format for a structured questionnaire.
   (g) Design the order and layout of the questionnaire.
2. Consider the questionnaire from the previous exercise. Decide the most appropriate sample size. Choose an appropriate sampling method from simple, stratified, cluster and quota sampling methods.

SCENARIO

We have already heard in Chapter 5 that Sister Brown has two main lines of enquiry:

- The likely effects on community nurse workloads of 5-day surgical units and day units (a quantitative exercise).

- She also intends to interview a sample of patients and their carers on their feelings about early discharge (a less structured approach).

From this broad beginning she has developed some working hypotheses:

1. Earlier discharge will increase the workload of the community nurse.
2. Early discharge patients and their carers will express anxiety about coping at home.

To check the first hypothesis Sister Brown needs to design a form for community nurses to record details of their visits over a certain period. She hopes, as a spin-off to the study, that the form could be refined for use on a regular basis as a quality assurance tool.

She decides that the interviews with patients and carers will be more of a pilot study, involving a sample of early discharge patients, and will therefore be semi-structured. A great deal of exploratory work has already been covered in her day-to-day visits. Sister Brown would like to continue the study into a larger survey with a structured questionnaire, when day surgery and 5-day stays are introduced to Ward 4, so that the effects on patients and carers can be properly evaluated.

Visiting times
The forms that Sister Brown designed to record visiting times are shown in Figures 7.21 and 7.22. She has chosen to collect data over a 2-month period for all surgical patients in the hospital. She is aiming for a return on around 90 patients. To achieve this she has had to obtain the co-operation of a wide circle of colleagues in the hospital and in the community. The clinical nurse managers in the community have agreed to collect the records from community nurses. A note explaining the purpose of the study has been circulated to all the community nurses beforehand.

As a check on the community data, Sister Jones has offered to provide data on the number of patients referred from different surgical areas for community nurse support. The data can be gathered from the referral forms completed by the hospital liaison sisters. Sister Jones has asked them to make duplicates of the forms over the 2-month period.

Some of the data collected by the forms will be used for exercises in Chapter 9 on data analysis.

Patients and carers
The subjects for semi-structured interviews are selected from the community nurse records. Sister Brown plans to approach around 20 patients who have been discharged after less than 5 days. We said earlier that Sister Brown will need the consent of the ethical committee. She will also need the consent of individual patients and their respective carers. The consent form she has drafted is shown in Figure 7.23.

Please complete all sections

Ward/hospital discharged from:

Date of discharge: _____

Date of first visit: _____

Date of final visit: _____

Operation: _____

Operation date:

Liaison form received: yes/no (delete as appropriate)

If patient treated in treatment room/general practitioner surgery by district nurse, use initials T/R in appropriate timings box.

If treatment given at general practitioner surgery by practice nurse, please indicate under comments.

Hospital assessment of treatment needs on referral:

District nurse assessment of needs:

Comments:

Figure 7.21 A form for recording details of community nurse visits – 1

Patient's name _____ General practitioner _____

Month	1	2	3	4	5	6	7	8	9	10	11	12	13	14	15	16
Minutes	a.m.p.m.	a.m.p.m.	a.m.p.m.	a.m.p.m.	a.m.p.m.	a.m.p.m.	a.m.p.m.	a.m.p.m.	a.m.p.m.	a.m.p.m.	a.m.p.m.	a.m.p.m.	a.m.p.m.	a.m.p.m.	a.m.p.m.	a.m.p.m.
Less than 15																
Up to 30																
Up to 50																
Up to 60																
60 +																

Month	17	18	19	20	21	22	23	24	25	26	27	28	29	30	31
Minutes	a.m.p.m.	a.m.p.m.	a.m.p.m.	a.m.p.m.	a.m.p.m.	a.m.p.m.	a.m.p.m.	a.m.p.m.	a.m.p.m.	a.m.p.m.	a.m.p.m.	a.m.p.m.	a.m.p.m.	a.m.p.m.	a.m.p.m.
Less than 15															
Up to 30															
Up to 50															
Up to 60															
60 +															

Figure 7.22 A form for recording details of community nurse visits – 2

SOUTHSHIRE HEALTH AUTHORITY
COMMUNITY SURVEY: COPING AT HOME AFTER SURGERY

Informed Consent Form

As community nurses, we are interested to find out how surgery patients and their carers cope at home after a short stay in hospital, and the kind of support they need.

We would, therefore, like to interview some patients and their main carers (if appropriate). Each interview would be conducted by a community nurse, Sister Brown, and would last no more than half an hour. All information will be treated confidentially both during and after the study. Sister Brown would be happy to discuss any questions you might have (Telephone 54321).

If you consent to take part in the study, we would be grateful if you could complete the tear-off slip below and give it to your local community nurse.

....

COMMUNITY SURVEY: COPING AT HOME AFTER SURGERY

This is to certify that ....(print name) CAN/CANNOT (please delete as appropriate) participate in the above-named study, and that I DO/DO NOT (please delete) give permission for information given in an interview to be recored in written form. I understand that all material will be treated as highly confidential by the researcher. I have been given the opportunity to ask any questions, and know that I am free to withdraw my consent at any time.

Signed   ....

Date   ....

Figure 7.23 An example of a consent form

In designing the interview schedule she must bear in mind that community nurses already have a tight time schedule – that is the theme of her study. She therefore keeps the schedules short and to the point. These are reproduced in Figures 7.24 and 7.25. Note that she has produced one schedule for patients and one for carers, because she realises she cannot gauge the feelings of the carer by asking the patient, and vice versa.

With the results of her interviews Sister Brown would be able to construct a structured questionnaire, with mainly closed questions, for use with a much larger sample. This could be used with patients from her own

COMMUNITY SURVEY: COPING AT HOME AFTER SURGERY

Patient Interview Schedule

1. How long were you in hospital?

2. Did you feel ready to come home?

3. Were you given details about your condition (if so, by whom)?

4. Do you feel you were given enough information?

5. Do you have a carer at home (if so, please give name and relationship)?

6. Do you have any particular problems coping at home
   (domestic arrangements, etc.)?

7. How will you manage?

8. Do you have any other worries?

9. Is there anything you think you need?

THANKS FOR YOUR HELP

Figure 7.24 Community survey interview schedule – 1

ward to evaluate the proposed changes. In this case the sample would be aggregated over time with successive patients.

REFERENCES

Hoinville G and Jowell R (1977) *Survey Research Practice*. London: Heinemann.
Macleod Clark J and Hockey L (1979) *Research for Nursing: A Guide for the Enquiring Nurse*. London: H M and M Publishers.
Macleod Clark J and Hockey L (eds.) (1988) *Further Research for Nursing: A New*

COMMUNITY SURVEY: COPING AT HOME AFTER SURGERY

Carer Interview Schedule

1. What is your relationship to the patient?

2. Did you feel ready to look after the patient at home?

3. Were you given details about the patient's condition (if so, by whom)?

4. Do you feel you were given enough information?

5. How much support do you need to give to the patient?

6. Do you have any particular problems coping at home (domestic arrangements, etc.)?

7. How will you manage?

8. Do you have any other worries?

9. Is there anything you think you need?

THANKS FOR YOUR HELP

Figure 7.25 Community survey interview schedule – 2

Guide for the Enquiring Nurse. London: Scutari Press.

Moser C A and Kalton G (1971) *Survey Methods in Social Investigations.* London: Heinemann.

Oppenheim A N (1966) *Questionnaire Design and Attitude Measurement.* London: Heinemann.

Wilson-Barnett J (ed.) (1983) *Nursing Research: Ten Studies in Patient Care.* Chichester: Wiley.

FURTHER READING

Cormack D F S (1984) *The Research Process in Nursing*, chs 9 and 11. Oxford: Blackwell.

Polit D and Hungler B (1983) *Nursing Research: Principles and Methods*, chs 7, 9 and 11. Philadelphia: J B Lippincott.

Treece E W and Treece J W (1977) *Elements of Research in Nursing*. New York: Mosby.

8

Qualitative Techniques

The purpose of this chapter is to discuss the advantages and disadvantages of different qualitative techniques, to explore some of the issues in qualitative research and to describe some of the ways of analysing qualitative data.

There are two main methods of collecting qualitative data:

Interview
Observation

INTERVIEW

Just as qualitative and quantitative methods were discussed earlier as being at either end of a continuum, so interviews range from *structured* to *unstructured*. Figure 8.1 explains how this affects the data collected.

Setting up the interviews needs to be carefully planned. When the people to be interviewed (called respondents) are first contacted a convenient and suitable time and place for the next meeting must be agreed. This may only be a preliminary visit to explain what is required, what is expected of the respondent and to gain consent. More than one interview may be necessary with each respondent, and if the researcher feels this is likely then he or she should be honest and say so. The respondents should, when consent is sought, be told clearly that they may withdraw from the study at any time.

It is a good idea to give them a letter explaining as simply as possible the purpose of the study and the name and telephone number of whom to contact if they have any queries or worries. The letter should also state that respondents are under no obligation to participate and that they may withdraw from the study at any time. If children or other vulnerable groups are involved, then permission must be sought from a responsible person.

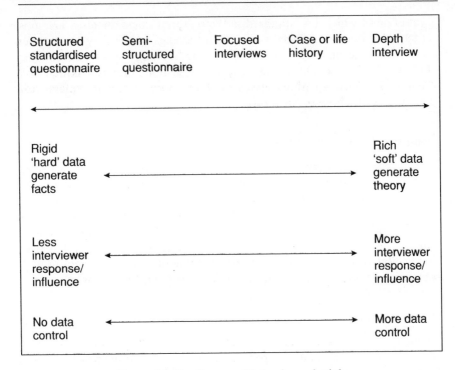

Figure 8.1 Continuum of interview schedule

STANDARDISED, STRUCTURED QUESTIONNAIRES

In this type of interview every respondent is asked exactly the same set of questions, with exactly the same wording and in the same order. The rationale for this is that by providing the same stimulus to each person interviewed the responses will be comparable. The person conducting the interviews will have less influence on the answers – as long as they stick to the questionnaire.

There are several problems with this type of interview:

1. Not all the people being interviewed will interpret the wording in the same way. This can be partly overcome by a good pilot study of the questionnaire before the main study commences. Wording should be clear and unambiguous and there should be no double-barrelled questions or complex sentences.
2. By providing a very rigid set of questions respondents may be forced into a very rigid set of answers.
3. Such an interview is extremely artificial. The questions being asked may not provide the opportunity for the respondent to say how he or she really feels about the issue being discussed.

Interviews which use standardised, structured questionnaires are most suitable for obtaining 'facts' rather than 'feelings'. Thus they can be seen as more to the quantitative end of the methodology spectrum, but they do have their place. Designing structured questionnaires is a skilled task. Chapter 7 discusses various survey methods more fully, and explains how to construct such research tools.

Semi-structured questionnaires

In this type of interview the interviewer is able to use more complex questions, and to 'probe' for more information. Semi-structured questionnaires all ask the same questions, but the approach is less rigid. The interviewer can rephrase the question if the respondent does not understand it, or clarify something which is not clear. Interviews that use questionnaires can provide information, such as the number of times someone has been in hospital, or the last time they visited the doctor, but they cannot provide data on how people felt about going into hospital, for example.

Focused interviews

A focused, or guided, interview is rather different. For this the researcher has a list of issues about the particular topic of the research which he or she wishes to cover, but the interview is much more like a conversation.

In this way topics can be discussed as they arise, and in the respondent's own words, rather than in the order and format prescribed on a questionnaire. A much wider range of data can be collected in this way, with much more depth. The respondent may raise issues about the topic which the interviewer had not thought of, or considered unimportant or unlikely. Data collected in this way are said to be much 'richer'.

Because of their nature, focused interviews can become rather painful or uncomfortable for respondent and interviewer. The interviewer needs to be quite skilled at behaving in a way which is non-directive, non-judgemental, but supportive.

Whereas a structured questionnaire has all the information recorded in coded form on the questionnaire itself this is only partly true of semi-structured questionnaires, and not at all for focused interviews. Tape recorders are invaluable here, and provided they are sensitively introduced and employed are increasingly well accepted. By using a tape recorder the researcher is freed from the task of writing copious notes and can concentrate on the respondent, watching for non-verbal as well as verbal cues in following up answers.

The tape recorder should not be placed in too conspicuous a position, and small microphones may be helpful. If respondents are embarrassed or hesitant about being recorded, more general conversation at the start of the interview can usually overcome this. Once a more relaxed atmosphere is established the tape recorder will generally be forgotten, and the interview proper can proceed.

Focused interviews are used to explore attitudes or beliefs. Although they can form the major part of a research design, focused interviews are also useful in constructing more formal questionnaires. By eliciting the perceptions and viewpoint of a small sample of research subjects, the researcher is guided on the questions and perhaps wording of a subsequent questionnaire to be administered to the research sample.

Whether the interview is the administration of a structured questionnaire or a focused interview, the researcher must keep certain things in mind.

First, even when the interview is conducted informally it is not a normal social interaction. The participants are probably strangers to each other, and the encounter will be transitory in nature. This can be an advantage, in that respondents may be more frank with someone they never expect to meet again. Differences in class, age, and sex between respondent and interviewer may affect the rapport that this technique requires. Also, the participants are not on an equal footing in that the respondent is the novice and the interviewer the expert in the situation.

Secondly, it may be difficult to keep the respondent to the point. Although some anecdotal or unrelated matter may be unavoidable the interviewer needs to stay in control of the interview. At the same time the interviewer must avoid giving – even when asked – advice, opinions or imposing his or her own perspective on the material the respondent is presenting.

Thirdly, interviews can take quite a long time. It is important to minimise distractions or interruptions from others not directly concerned; other members of the respondent's family, for instance. The time and place of the interview should be arranged bearing this in mind.

There are two other types of interviews that are worth knowing about, but that are not really suitable for the inexperienced or first-time researcher.

Case or life histories

A case or life history is similar to a focused interview in that it allows the respondents to give their own accounts, and in their own words. However, case or life histories are more autobiographical and will have much wider-ranging subject matter. Case histories can be of events, organisations or specific settings, as well as of individuals. Thus a case history could be of one family's experience with a disabled child over a period of several years, or with the establishment, organisation and achievements of a new health clinic. Interviews are obviously ongoing, being conducted over a long period of time, and may involve interviews with more than one person.

This kind of study obviously requires a great deal of commitment on the part of the researcher, and indeed more than one researcher could be involved in the work.

Depth interview

In a depth interview there is more interaction between participants. This may develop almost to the point of counselling, with the researcher reflecting and clarifying what the respondent says. The point of this is to get at 'hidden' or 'difficult' data, particularly with deviant or unusual subjects, and the interview can therefore be very difficult to conduct. Depth interviews can be useful as a prelude to formulating the schedule for focused interviews.

OBSERVATION

Observation can be classified into two types: observing specific events and observing situations.

Observing specific events

In this type of observation the researcher will have decided beforehand exactly what he or she is looking for. This is likely to be some kind of 'count' of things, such as the number of times the ward sister answers the telephone in a given period, or how often patients in a day hospital initiate conversation with a nurse.

Observing situations

The researcher may observe the setting in order to understand what is happening. This may be:

- to find the reason for particular events;
- to test a theory or hypothesis around which the research is designed;
- to generate theory.

There are two points to make here. First, both types of observation may be the only method of data collection, but they are more likely to be used in conjunction. For example, observation to understand the organisation of a ward may bring to light the fact that the ward sister spends a great deal of time on the telephone, in which case observation which specifically counted and timed this activity could follow. Conversely, if observation started by concentrating on this telephone-time the next stage could be to see how this affects the rest of the ward staff.

Secondly, the researcher has to decide on the role he or she will adopt

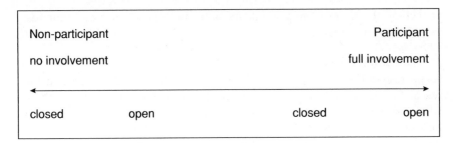

Figure 8.2 Range of observer roles

– in other words how much the observer will take part in what is going on. Figure 8.2 shows the range of involvement. in research settings. Each situation has its advantages and disadvantages, and the researcher must decide which is the most appropriate for their particular study.

Non-participant
As a non-participant the researcher takes on no role or task other than that of observer. Not only does this relate to activities – such as helping with bed-making! – but also as far as possible not engaging in anything that changes or distorts the setting, which may include conversation with those being observed. The objective is to become a 'fly on the wall'.

Non-participant observation may be 'open' or 'closed'. As this implies, open is when the subjects know they are being observed, closed is when they do not – or do not know the true purpose.

The question you may be asking about non-participant observation is 'don't people change their behaviour once they know you are watching?' This is called the Hawthorne effect, after a famous series of studies carried out in the United States. In fact, people usually become accustomed to observation quite quickly. In any case, it is difficult to sustain a different pattern of behaviour over a long period of time and in a consistent fashion. Open observation does have the advantage that the appearance of the researcher at meetings and in various locations is explained, and people will not be surprised if the researcher asks questions or looks at records.

Closed non-participant observation is more difficult for several reasons. If the closed context has been achieved by giving a different reason from the true one, or subjects are unaware that they are being observed, then ethical issues arise. In practical terms how can subjects be observed without their knowledge? Public places such as waiting areas or canteens do not present too much of a problem as the researcher can become one of the crowd, although considerable skill and discretion over note-taking will be necessary, but what about a clinical area? In some research one-way mirrors or hidden cameras have been used. Once again the ethical considerations are major; also, such techniques may not allow adequate data collection, as the most important and informative events may occur just out of sight or earshot.

Participant observation

Some research settings and questions can best be investigated when the researcher takes part in the setting itself. Thus if the research is about what topics of conversation are initiated by patients, the researcher could become one of the ward team. Obviously the researcher has to negotiate a role in the setting prior to, or immediately upon starting the data collection. What that role is will depend upon whether the observation is open or closed – as in non-participant observation, meaning whether the subjects know what, or if, research is being carried out. Open participation may have an effect on the behaviour of others, but the researcher will have more understanding of what form this takes.

He or she must not, however, lose sight of the observer role, remaining objective and impartial and not taking any action that will affect the behaviour or structure of the setting. On the other hand the advantages of open, non-participant observation are enhanced. Others in the setting will tend to forget the researcher's 'other' role while accepting their presence and questions.

Closed participant observation may be the only method possible if the research setting is somewhat contentious, for instance with drug addicts or other groups who might resent being the subject of investigation. Apart from the ethical problems here the role the researcher adopts has to be very carefully chosen and scrupulously maintained. Again, the researcher must remain objective and not allow the assumed role to influence or disturb the behaviour of others.

Clearly, observation studies require tact, sensitivity and a great deal of delicacy if they are to be successful.

One-way mirrors

Observations can be carried out by the use of one-way mirrors, but as stated previously there are ethical dilemmas here. If you are observing a situation in which respondents are unaware of this, then you are guilty of invasion of privacy and exploitation. On the other hand, to what extent would their behaviour change if they knew they were being observed?

RECORDING THE DATA

Recording the observation as completely as possible is very important. Notes should be made on the spot when this is feasible, or as soon after events occur as possible. For researchers working in a closed context this may mean frequent trips to the toilet, or frequent recourse to a cupboard!

How and what to record

The first stage in observing a situation will be largely unstructured. The purpose will be to get the 'feel', notice patterns or routines of behaviour. This stage may provide data to define classification or degree, or to start ideas. The second stage will be more structured. Confirmation and checking of concepts identified in the first stage takes place, or the objective and focus of the observation becomes narrowed. Notes will vary according to the stage and purpose of the observation. However, you should keep three sets of notes.

Field notes
These are the record of the observation itself, and should be made at the time or very soon after leaving the setting. The example below is of a nurse–patient interaction:

> *Nurse (approaching bed)*   'Time to get up Mrs Jones'
> *Mrs Jones (eyes shut)*   'I don't feel well enough'
> *Nurse (draws screens)*   'I'm sure you'll feel better out of bed'

> Nurse takes clothes out of locker. Mrs Jones struggles to sit up, then falls back onto pillow. Nurse assists Mrs Jones to sit up. Nurse begins to help Mrs Jones out of nightdress. Neither speaks.

Field notes should be in 'native language' – that is, as used by participants, and verbatim if possible. If the observation is of action, not speech, then be as specific as possible.

Personal field work journal
A journal is used to record significant events such as meetings attended, or changes to the organisation or staffing of the setting.

Ideas on analysis and interpretation
As the research proceeds you may get some clues about how to analyse the data. Similarities (or differences) may suggest concepts, categories or explanations worth pursuing. For instance, the observation recorded in the example could lead to two different concepts:

1. Nurse strategies to obtain patient compliance.
2. Token resistance by patient to demonstrate independence.

Write such ideas down, or you may forget them.

ANALYSING QUALITATIVE DATA

As with deciding on what method to use to study a particular research question, the analysis undertaken will depend on the purpose of the research.

Interviews

No matter what kind of interviews have been conducted, considerable work is necessary before the actual analysis can begin. Structured and semi-structured questionnaires must be scrutinised and coded. Responses to open-ended questions will have to be classified prior to coding. Depending on the size of the sample the data can be put on to computer for analysis, or analysed manually. The researcher is looking for relationships between the variables of the study; for instance, does the age of a diabetic patient correlate with diet compliance? (The variables here are 'age' and 'diet compliance'.) Statistical techniques will be required to establish the validity of such relationships. The analysis of questionnaires is discussed more fully in Chapter 9.

Interviews that have been tape-recorded must be typed up to form a transcript. As a rule of thumb, transcribing will take three times as long as the original interview! Interviews not tape-recorded must be checked for clarity and probably transcribed also to allow analysis. Always make three copies of a transcript, then if disaster strikes you will not lose all your data. Put the original tapes or notes away in a safe place – do not use them as working documents for the analysis.

Observation notes

As with interview data, preparation is required before analysis is started. Make sure your notes are in the right sequence and if the writing is not clear, type the notes into a transcript, making three copies. You may wish to make separate copies of conversations you have recorded, so that you can make a preliminary analysis of both conversation and events before seeing how one reinforces or is different from the other. Have you recorded the outcome of any meetings you attended, or followed up any loose ends which remained when you left the research setting?

Analysis

The next step is to read the transcripts through at least twice. Does anything significant strike you? Are the same phrases, actions or attitudes recurring? If so, can you classify them – do some of the responses or events seem to express guilt, or frustration and so on? Consult your field work journal and your 'ideas' notes. Is there anything there to give you a lead?

How you proceed from here is a matter of personal choice. Some researchers use highlighter pens to mark categories and concepts on the portions of transcript. Thus all sections which refer to 'guilt' could be highlighted in red, 'frustration' in blue, and so on. The transcript can be scrutinised for other concepts or sub-categories of the existing ones. Always keep one transcript unmarked.

Another method is to cut out the parts of a transcript referring to a particular concept, such as 'fear', glue each one onto a blank sheet of paper, then file according to classification. If some sections can be classi-fied in more than one way, then the second copy of the transcript comes into service.

Yet another way is to copy the relevant parts of the transcript onto postcards, then sort these into piles according to classification.

The purpose of all this is to get at the underlying meaning of the situ-ation for respondents, to see what concepts lie behind the answers they gave, the events you saw. It could be that your literature search provided a framework which supports your findings and places them into a theo-retical context that explains or clarifies the particular research question you are attempting to answer.

If you started out to test a particular hypothesis, the data analysis will be for the purpose of supporting, refuting or modifying that hypothesis.

Glaser and Strauss are generally regarded as the most prominent propo-nents of what is known as 'Generating Grounded Theory' (Glaser and Strauss, 1968). This means, in its simplest form, looking for theory to explain the data in the data itself, rather than looking to existing theory into which the data has to be 'fitted'.

Once concepts begin to emerge and a tentative theory has been formu-lated the researcher returns to the data to test the theory out, and to see how the theory must be modified to fit the data that has been gathered. Further data is then collected, but this time only that which is relevant to the theory generated is gathered. Data collection and analysis is thus a sequential process.

Whatever method you choose to analyse your data, you should continue to scrutinise the material until you feel that no new concepts, ideas or interpretations are left. The theory or framework that you are using for your analysis should explain all of your data. If there are some things which seem to contradict this, ask yourself why this is. 'Deviant cases', that is instances which are different from the rest, should not be ignored. By attempting to understand why certain respondents or situations are atypical you may reach a fuller understanding of the way in which the analysis explains the data, and of the theoretical interpretation.

SCENARIO

Observation

The team on Ward 4 feel it would be useful to find out what kinds of things patients worry about on going home after having had an operation. That would help the ward staff in preparing patients for discharge, perhaps by developing some information sheets or other material. However, there is not really very much time to devote to the research, the ward is busy and no one can take time out to conduct a large study. Is it possible to carry out research at the same time as working on the ward?

Given the limitations of time and expedience, participant observation in a closed context is probably the most suitable method. The ward has a system of patient allocation, so it is suggested that Student Nurse Green should observe patients she is allocated, noting how they behave and what they say while she is caring for them. Hopefully she will be able to pick out the features which relate to the operation and treatment and how patients feel about what effect this will have on their lives after discharge. There could be a problem with recording data, but as nurses are forever writing things down on charts and care-plans Nurse Green hopes that this will be possible without being too obvious to patients. She will, however, have to look at these records as soon as she goes off duty to make sure that they are as complete as possible before she has forgotten what she observed. Recall falls off sharply with the passage of time. Student Nurse Green will also be able to record what patients ask the doctors on the ward round, sit in on case conferences and discharge meetings, look at medical and nursing notes and record which other agencies are brought in, such as the social work department.

Student Nurse Green will need to analyse the data sequentially, checking and refining her ideas, and exploring difficult or 'deviant' cases of patients who seem to have different views from those most commonly expressed. As the study proceeds, the data she collects will become more focused and directed to particular concepts as they emerge.

Although Student Nurse Green will be attempting to generate theory from the data itself, she will need to make use of established theoretical concepts in order to provide a framework for her analysis. The literature on stress and coping that the team have found will be useful here.

Exercise

Simply watching what goes on sounds easy, but if the observation is for research it has to done carefully and with some planning. Try the exercises given below; you will find them quite entertaining and very interesting!

The object of this exercise is to report, interpret and analyse a social event from the perspective of the people involved, using unstructured observation or interview methods. Select a social event in your work setting in which you already share some of the cultural norms, and to which you have access. For instance, you might look at the ways in which fellow nurses 'negotiate' their relationships with other professionals, or the inter-action at ward rounds.

Decide on a setting for the observation. You will need to negotiate your own access and obtain permission and remember that if clients or patients are involved ethical approval will be necessary. Observation is carried out over a period of several days or weeks depending on the time available. Data should be analysed sequentially with data collection, so that the field of inquiry is increasingly narrowed and focused and theoretical concepts checked out as they emerge from analysis.

Write a report of at least 1000 words which covers:

1. A brief introduction to the setting.
2. Justification of the method used.
3. How the exercise was conducted.
4. A description of the social event, including passages of dialogue where appropriate.
5. Interpretation and discussion of results grounded theoretically in the data and in the light of other existing theories.
6. An evaluation of methods and findings of the exercise.

Group exercise

In a group setting, divide into teams of twos or threes. Each team decides on a setting for undertaking non-participant observation. A public setting such as a waiting area is best, but the tutor should obtain permission from the relevant staff beforehand. Each team observes their setting for about an hour, recording any gestures, talk or movement that occurs. At this stage only basic observational data is recorded with as little inference as possible. Team members do not confer with each other until the end of the observation period, when they compare notes and try to suggest some pattern, explanation or theory for the events they have observed.

If this is a class activity the material collected is analysed, looking for the sociological features of the situation, the categories and concepts that are suggested, the 'roles' of participants and the 'rules' governing inter-action, including departures from these 'rules'. The data will be used to support the theoretical ideas.

REFERENCE

Glaser B and Strauss A (1968) *The Discovery of Grounded Theory: Strategies for qualitative research*. Chicago: Aldine.

FURTHER READING

Field P A and Morse J M (1985) *Nursing Research. The Application of Qualitative Approaches*. London: Croom Helm.
Fox D J (1976) *Fundamentals of Research in Nursing*, 3rd edn, ch. 12. New York: Appleton-Century-Crofts.

Hughes J A (1976) *Sociological Analysis: Methods of Discovery*, ch. 5. Walton-on-Thames: Thomas Nelson and Sons.

Krausz E and Miller S (1974) *Social Research and Design*. London: Longman.

Macleod Clark J and Hockey L (1979) *Research for Nursing: a Guide for the Enquiring Nurse*. London: H and M Publishers.

Moser C A and Kalton G (1979) *Survey Methods in Social Investigation*, 2nd edn, chs 10 and 12. London: Heinemann Educational Books.

Munhall P L and Oiler C J (1986) *Nursing Research: a Qualitative Perspective*. Conn: Appleton-Century-Crofts.

Oppenheim A N (1966) *Questionnaire Design and Attitude Measurement*. London: Heinemann Educational Books.

Treece E W and Treece J W (1986) *Elements of Research in Nursing*, chs 17 and 19. St Louis: Mosby.

Verhonick P and Seaman C (1978) *Research Methods for Undergraduate Students in Nursing*, ch. 6. New York: Appleton-Century-Crofts.

9

Data Analysis

If, as we have argued throughout this book, research is a problem-solving process, then analysis of the data helps to see if we have the evidence to solve our problem, the answer to our question. At the end of any research study we are faced with a mass of undigested data. Data analysis techniques are simply a means of organising or summarising the data to look for patterns and order. This applies whether you have used quantitative or qualitative data collection methods. In the first case you have numbers and in the second case words, but systematic approaches are needed in both cases to make sense of the data.

Systems for analysing qualitative data have already been described in Chapter 8. This chapter will be concerned with quantitative data and statistical approaches to analysis. The approaches that will be discussed would apply to data from experimental or survey research studies.

Many people find this the most off-putting stage in research, probably because of a fear of maths that survives from school. When you have some results from your own research, however, statistical techniques can appear less threatening. They are, after all, common-sense tools to bring some order out of chaos, and you don't have to be a mathematical genius to use them. We do not regard ourselves as mathematical geniuses, simply people who have gained understanding through coping with our own data and becoming more confident with practice. We therefore feel able to appreciate the level of difficulties that other people experience when confronting data analysis and offer our own coping strategies. You could call this a 'Mickey Mouse' guide to statistics! It is correct, but we have tried to make it as straightforward and understandable as possible. There are plenty of examples to demonstrate techniques and exercises at the end of the book to help you to gain confidence.

DEFINITIONS

The word 'statistics' has more than one meaning. It can mean:

- the data itself;
- the activity of analysing the data; or
- specific statistical tests,

and each of these aspects will be explored in that order in this chapter. We shall therefore be talking about statistics at two main levels: the level of *interpreting* data (research reports and official statistics); and the level of *doing* statistics.

OFFICIAL STATISTICS

Official statistics can be a valuable source of information in research in several different ways:

1. You can consult the various digests of statistics as part of your literature search (see Chapter 3) for baseline information on the population to be studied. For example, in a study within psychiatric nursing you might want to quote the annual rate of admission to and discharge of patients from long-stay hospitals over a given period.
2. Reading official statistics can often generate ideas for research – puzzling patterns and connections between things that you would like to explain in more detail. An example might be the connection between health and occupation or class that is published in official statistical tables.
3. The figures themselves can also be analysed further in a quasi-experimental study (see Chapter 6 on experimental methods). Studying figures before and after a change in law or policy, for instance community care policies, could yield new insights into the effectiveness of that change.

There are various forms of data collection used by the government. They can be categorised in the following way:

1. *Census.* Data on households collected nationwide every 10 years. Useful baseline data, although it can be several years before all the results are published.
2. *Registers of electors.*
3. *Vital registration.* Births, deaths, marriages, divorces.
4. *Surveys.*
   (a) Continuous (annual/biannual – 10 000 per annum): general household survey; family expenditure; national food survey; labour force survey; new earnings survey.
   (b) *Ad hoc,* e.g. women's employment; family formation; national dwelling and housing; industrial relations; royal commissions, etc.
5. *Administrative structures* e.g. DHSS – hospital bed-days, number of doctors, prescriptions, Chief MOH report, crime statistics, unemployment, education.

Most of these statistics are the by-product of the book-keeping data of various government departments published for general use. For an index or guide to possible statistical sources of information in your area of interest consult the *Guide to Official Statistics* published by the Central Statistical Office (CSO). Perhaps the most digestible form of government statistics comes in publications such as *Social Trends* and *Population Trends* from the CSO which will be available in most libraries. These are published yearly and summarise data from many sources with useful commentary and discussion. The topics include population, housing, environment, education, employment and income, as well as health and social services information.

Official statistics do need to be approached with some caution, however. There may be problems associated with the collection of the data that need to be taken into account in interpretation.

There might be technical problems such as a high non-response rate which biased the sample. The terms used might not have been defined consistently over time. For example, the census definitions for bathrooms have changed over time so it is difficult to see if there is any real change in people's living conditions.

Other problems might occur with the meaning of terms and categories. What are the assumptions and values behind the statistics? Who selected the categories? Who defined the terms? Apparently 'hard' data such as cause of death can, in fact, be decided with some discretion by doctors, police and coroners.

ANALYSING DATA

When it comes to doing statistics we would suggest a simple procedure to guide you. You can 'ease' yourself gently into a set of data by following this series of steps:

Data——→Table——→Graph——→Statistics

These steps will be demonstrated through examples in the rest of the chapter. The procedure is the same whether you are analysing one variable or more. The statistics can increase in level of complexity and sophistication. We will be concerned mainly with descriptive statistics, deriving figures that describe patterns in the data. The majority of nursing research studies report results at this level. Some use inferential statistics (that is, the statistics are used to infer, for instance, a causal relationship between variables) and more advanced statistical procedures such as regression analysis. Our treatment of these methods will be more at the level of interpretation – how to interpret this kind of result when you encounter it in a research report.

WORKED EXAMPLES

In order to understand the processes involved we suggest that you carry out the steps outlined below. Most could be done 'by hand' but you might prefer to use a calculator. In practice, if you were involved in a research project a computer programme could do all the calculations you need in minutes, but it helps if you understand the process first.

Let's start by generating some real data on which to practise. How much sleep do you get compared with other people? Jot down as accurately as possible the times you went to bed and the times that you got up, to the nearest half-hour, over the last 7 days. Then collect the same information from a few other people, perhaps members of your family or colleagues at work, noting in addition their sex, approximate age and any other details that you think are interesting. We should point out at this stage that this exercise is for demonstration purposes only and will not follow strict statistical rules like sampling.

We could start summarising the data by seeing on how many occasions people went to bed by midnight, or had more than 8 hours' sleep. To do this count up the total number of bedtimes or nights of sleep from all the people in your sample (this should be the number of people multiplied by 7, for the number of days you are covering). Now count the number of occasions you are interested in, whether it is bedtimes by midnight or more than 8 hours' sleep. To compare the people who went to bed later or had less sleep, you simply calculate the remainder from your total. An example is given at the end of the chapter.

The results can be made even clearer by converting the raw data to percentages because this puts the results on a standard scale and makes comparisons easier. To convert your data into a percentage, make a fraction from the occasions of interest over the total and multiply by 100.

$$\frac{\text{bedtimes by midnight}}{\text{total bedtimes}} \times 100 = \% \text{ bedtimes by midnight}$$

TABLES

The next step in our step-by-step procedure is to express our results in table form. In the example above we would present the numbers as we have in Table 9.1.

This type of table is called a frequency table – in other words, a table that shows how frequently certain categories occur. With only the two categories of answer, in this case, by midnight, after midnight, or Yes and No, it is usually enough to quote the results in your report without needing a table. When you have several categories of answer it becomes more necessary to communicate the results through a table.

A frequency table would be useful if we wanted to summarise the data

Table 9.1 Frequency table of bedtimes data – 1

Bedtimes	Number
By midnight	24
After midnight	11
Total	35

by bedtimes or hours of sleep, from the earliest to the latest, the longest to the shortest, etc. Notice in the example in Table 9.2 that it is usual to give both the raw figure and the percentage.

Table 9.2 Frequency table of bedtimes data — 2;
Table to show hours of sleep per night

Hours	Number	%
6–7	10	28
8–9	16	46
10–11	9	26
Total	35	100

Graphs

The tables in all our examples could next be translated into graphic form, such as a bar chart, histogram or pie chart. The advantages here are that the human eye and brain seem to assimilate information more easily in visual form. If a graphic display does not communicate results more clearly than text or table, then it has not been properly used.

Figures 9.1 and 9.2 show the data from the table in Table 9.2 converted into bar chart and pie chart form. Both illustrate how much more effective a graph can be than a table in communicating results.

If you have collected your own data, try converting your data to charts and compare with our examples.

Statistics

Data that has been presented in table or graph form can in turn be summarised by just one or more statistics.

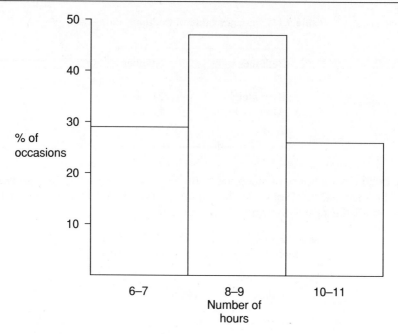

Figure 9.1 Bar chart of range of hours of sleep per night.

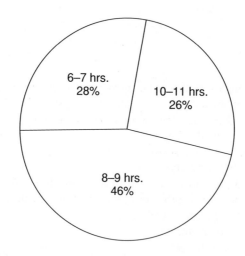

Figure 9.2 Pie chart of range of hours of sleep per night

Averages

The first summary statistic that is usually calculated is an average. There are three different types of average to choose from, largely depending on the type of measurement that was used:

1. *Mode* – the value that occurs most often (the most common value).
2. *Median* – the value that is exactly half way in the order of values (the central observation).
3. *Mean* – the sum of the value of all observations divided by the number of observations.

The mean is the average most familiar from schooldays and everyday calculations, but it is not always the most appropriate. For example, it was once quoted on a current affairs programme that the average salary is £20 000. This may be a sore point, but the majority of us do not seem to approach anything like that figure in our annual salary. The point is that it does not take many salaries of £100 000 or higher to distort the average if you are calculating a mean. Common sense suggests that it might be more accurate to find a figure that the majority of us receive (the mode) or some figure half way along the scale from the lowest to the highest (the median).

Exercises

What is the *mode* from the following set of salaries?

    £6000
    £8000
    £10 000
    £10 000
    £10 000
    £12 000
    £12 000
    £14 000
    £16 000

Answer: £10 000 is the mode, as it occurs most often.

What is the *mean* here?

    £8 000
    £10 000
    £12 000
    £14 000
    £16 000

Answer: The mean is £12 000.

And the *median* for this set?

   £6000
   £7000
   £9000
   £13 000
   £15 000
   £15 000

Answer: £11 000. As there are an even number of figures, you need to calculate the midway point, in this case between the third value (£9000) and the fourth (£13 000).

What do you think would be the most appropriate average for the bedtime data?

We have already shown in the bar chart in Figure 9.1 that 8–9 hours is the usual amount of time for sleep. This is the *mode*, and probably the easiest and most sensible summary statistic for this data. In fact, if we calculated the median and the mean we would also come up with somewhere between 8 and 9 hours.

As a general rule of thumb use the mode with a simple set of data like this as the most common-sense way of expressing an average. With a larger and more complete data set, the median is a very reliable average, but if you are likely to be applying statistical tests then calculation of the mean will be necessary.

A more technical explanation is that the choice of average depends on the level of measurement of the data. The mean can only be used with 'continuous data', that is measures in order on a continuous scale, such as salary or temperature (also called parametric data). With 'discrete data' (or non-parametric data) the mode or median is more appropriate. This is where the measures are in discrete categories and not in numerical order, for instance different professions or days of the week.

Standard deviation

If data are continuous and could be represented on a graph as a smooth symmetrical curve, then all the data can be summarised by just two statistics – the mean and the standard deviation. The standard deviation is a measure of the shape and distribution of the data represented by the curve, and shows by how much the scores deviate from the mean. It is the most commonly used measure of variability in data. It is useful for locating an individual score relative to others and in comparing samples.

If, for example, we measured the heights of a large section of the adult population and mapped these onto a graph, we would arrive at a shape something like that in Figure 9.3.

This is like a smoothed-out histogram or bar chart, and it is the typical

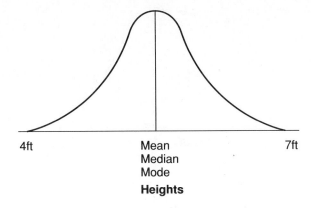

4ft   Mean   7ft
                Median
                Mode
                Heights

Figure 9.3 Normal curve for measures of height

symmetrical or 'normal' curve that has been observed for measures of
human characteristics. There is a large range of measures, with a large
proportion of them around the central observation. In the example of
height the measures range from 4 feet to 7 feet, but the majority are
around the 5'5" mark – the average.

We should point out that the word 'normal' has a precise technical
meaning here. The notion of normal distribution is fundamental to the
statistics of sampling, where some sort of estimation or probabilities are
involved. Probability statistics will be discussed later under the heading
of 'Inferential statistics'.

As Figure 9.3 shows, in a normal curve the mean, median and mode
averages are identical and fall at the central point. If the curve was
'skewed' or has more than one peak then the mean, median and mode
would probably differ. The median would be a more reliable indicator,
but the mean would be needed for statistical tests. Most statistical tests,
however, assume that the measures follow a normal curve.

Figure 9.4 shows that on a normal curve the first standard deviation
falls at the point either side of the centre where the curve changes shape.
The standard deviation is a more accurate way of expressing the curve
than a measure of range, because it is not so influenced by extreme values at
either end of the curve. In the example of heights if one or two people were
more than 8 feet tall this would give a false impression of the range. The
standard deviation is useful in statistics because it conforms to certain rules.
From Figure 9.4 it can be seen that 68% (two-thirds) of the observations in
the curve fall between one standard deviation either side of the mean, and
95% between two standard deviations either side of the mean.

These regularities in data can be used to predict and plan services and
are the basis of disciplines such as community health. The principles are
applied in the field of educational testing, for instance, where IQ tests

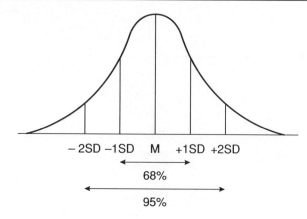

Figure 9.4 Normal curve for IQ measures showing standard deviations

such as the 11-plus exam have been used to stream children in secondary education. If the mean IQ was 100 then children with a score higher than one standard deviation above the mean at 115 would be considered grammar school material. Those 2.5% achieving above 130 or two standard deviations would be considered gifted.

At the other end of the scale, children and adults scoring less that 85 or one standard deviation below the mean on an IQ test have traditionally been labelled as having a learning disability. The 2.5% below two standard deviations were seen as severely mentally disabled. From such percentages it has been possible to calculate the incidence of severe learning disability in the population and plan the size of necessary provision and services.

Calculating the standard deviation

As we said earlier, the scope of this chapter is to do with the *interpretation* of statistics. If you need to calculate standard deviations for your own data we suggest you consult a statistician or one of the references listed at the end of the chapter.

TWO OR MORE VARIABLES

In this chapter a simple procedure for analysing data by following a series of steps has been suggested:

Data——→Table——→Graph——→Statistics

As we shall now demonstrate, the same procedure applies when you are analysing more than one variable.

Data

In a survey of perceptions of health, respondents were asked:

'Do you think you should make any changes in your life-style to benefit
your health?'
177 said 'Yes' and 70 said 'No'.

In analysing this or any data, it is a good idea to start with a list of
questions that you want to ask of the data. Your original hypothesis should
be the starting point. You might want to verify, for instance, whether there
was a difference in results between different ages, between men and
women, etc.

Tables

When you are cross-checking categories of more than one variable you
can organise the frequencies of the data into a contingency table (also
called cross-tabulation).

To continue the example of the survey on perceptions of health, we
might be interested in whether there was a difference between how men
and women answered the question 'Do you think you should make any
changes in your life-style to benefit your health?'. The contingency table
in Figure 9.5 shows the breakdown of Yes and No answers by gender.

A computer program would produce a table like this from your data
in an instant. If you have to do your data analysis by hand then you are
limited to rather more labour-intensive methods, such as sorting all your
questionnaires into two piles – one for men and one for women – and
then counting how many in each pile said Yes, and how many said No.

Notice how in Figure 9.5 converting the raw figures into percentages

	Women	Men
Yes	125 (78%)	52 (60%)
No	35 (22%)	35 (40%)
	160 (100%)	87 (100%)

Figure 9.5 Necessary changes in life-style perceived by men and women

Table 9.3 Hours of sleep of a small sample of people over a week

Person	Age	Mon	Tue	Wed	Thu	Fri	Sat	Sun
A	44	6	7	6	7	8	8	7
B	40	7	7	6	7	6	8	8
C	17	9	9	8	7	10	10	8
D	15	9	9	8	9	10	11	8
E	13	10	10	10	10	9	9	9

helps to highlight the relative proportions of the groups, especially if there are uneven numbers in the groups. In this case there were almost twice as many women as men. This was not a biased sample, however. As it was a sample of nurses it was fairly representative of the population.

If there is a pattern in the data this should be revealed in the table. In Figure 9.5 does the pattern of response differ between men and women, that is, as one set of responses increases, does the other set decrease? In this case there does seem to be a tendency for women to say they will change their life-style more than men, although more than half of both groups were willing to change.

We can demonstrate the process of cross-tabulation with an example from the bedtimes data. Let us start with the raw data in Table 9.3 and ask the question: 'Is there a difference between teenagers and adults in

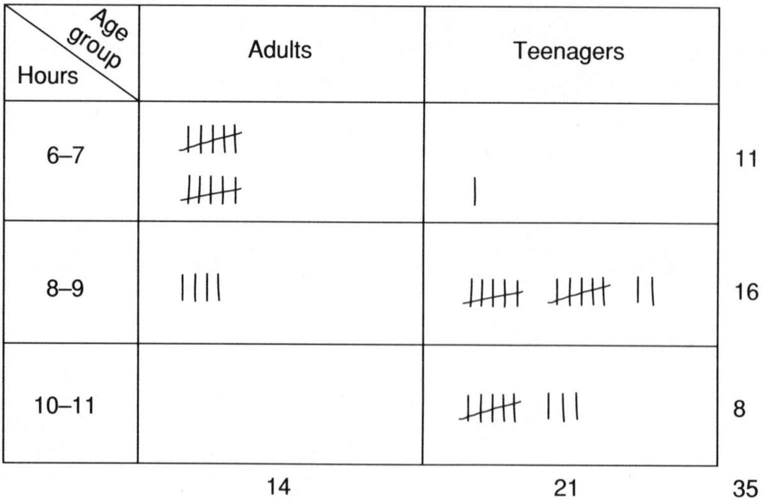

Figure 9.6 Tally of differences in amount of sleep between teenagers and adults over a week

Table 9.4 Differences in amount of sleep between adults and teenagers over a week

Hours	Adults	Teenagers	Total
6–7	10	1	11
8–9	4	12	16
10–11	0	8	8
Total	14	21	35

the amount of sleep they have?' The table can be constructed by tallying the different amounts of sleep over the week, between the two groups, as shown in Figure 9.6. The final tally appears in Table 9.4. Is there a difference between teenagers and adults?

Graphs

Variables measured by continuous or parametric scales can be plotted onto a graph in a *scatter plot*. For example, we might hypothesise that there is a relationship between length of service and salary, both of which are on a continuous scale and could be plotted onto a graph to see whether there is a link. It could be that both variables will increase; as one goes up so does the other; or that as one goes up the other goes down; or that there will be no connection at all. In the fictitious example in Figure 9.7 it does indeed look as though salary increases with longer service!

The variables of age and hours of sleep used in the contingency table in Table 9.4 are also continuous variables, even though we divided them into two (a *dichotomy*) or three groups for the table. We could plot the data onto a graph and look for a pattern. If there is one it should show even more clearly in a scatter plot. The trend should be that the older the person, the less sleep they get. There are not really enough cases over a wide range of ages in our data set, however, to get a true pattern.

Statistics

The statistic for summarising data in frequency tables with more than one variable is called the 'chi-squared test' (or χ^2). Because it is used with discrete groups or categories in tables it is a non-parametric test. It assesses whether there is a pattern or link between the variables in the table and therefore helps to test hypotheses. In Table 9.5 is presented the data from Figure 9.5 together with the chi-squared statistic which should help us to

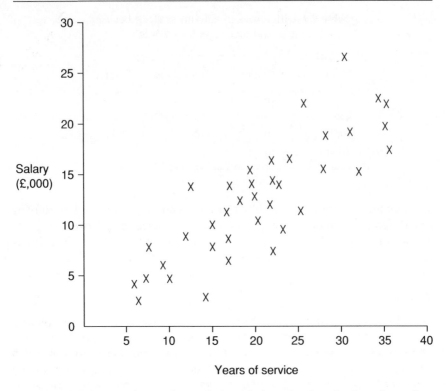

Figure 9.7 Scatter plot to show relationship between length of service and salary

decide whether there is a difference between men's and women's views on changing lifestyles for health as hypothesised. The chi-squared test has been used with a 2 × 2 table here, but can be used with larger tables.

Table 9.5 Necessary changes in life-style perceived by men and women, with chi-squared statistic

	Women	Men
Yes	125	52
	(78%)	(60%)
No	35	35
	(22%)	(40%)
Total	160	87
	(100%)	(100%)

Chi-squared = 7.85

The principle behind chi-squared is to test whether differences in the data are real or simply due to chance. If they are 'real', the hypothesis is supported and we can say we have a 'statistically significant result'. 'Significance' is used in this way, not in the everyday sense of 'important' or 'remarkable', but in a narrower statistical sense that will be discussed more fully later.

The figure of 7.85 in our example is the result of the chi-squared equation. This figure must in turn be checked against a table for the chi-squared test to see if it is statistically significant. The figure is, in fact, significant which means that the table shows a link between gender and attitudes towards change in lifestyles. In other words, we have some sound evidence for the hypothesis that women are more likely to say they will make changes in their lifestyle for the sake of their health.

We do not need to go into the details of the calculations of the chi-squared test here. You can get that from the Further Reading listed on p. 137. As we have said before it is more important in the first instance to be able to interpret such statistics when you encounter them in nursing studies.

Inferential statistics
The chi-squared test is an example of inferential statistical tests which infer the probabilities that the results from your sample are typical of the population as a whole. The results of tests like this are often expressed in a probability statement. You may have read studies which said something like: 'significance level $p < 0.01$' or 'the results were statistically significant at the 0.05 level of confidence'. This means that no more than once (0.01) or five times (0.05) in 100 would you get these results if chance factors alone were operating. You can therefore be 99% (0.01) or 95% (0.05) confident that the results were due to your intervention, your independent variable. In other words, you can accept your experimental hypothesis and reject the null hypothesis. It's a bit like the odds for betting in horse racing.

The usual levels for accepting significance are 0.01 and 0.05. With most data 0.05 is acceptable but if you need to be cautious then the level should be set at 0.01 or even 0.001. In clinical trials, for instance, you would need to be very sure that treatment was effective before introducing it into practice, especially if there were possible harmful effects. The lower the probability value the more confident you can be with the results.

Some computer programs for data analysis will print out a probability value to compare with the levels of statistical significance. In a study of student nurses' attitudes, for example, the value given for differences in attitudes between the beginning and end of the course was $p = 0.04$. You can see that it is statistically significant because it is below the $p = 0.05$ level and therefore lends support to the hypothesis that training will influence nurses' attitudes.

The chi-squared test is used to describe contingency tables. *Correlation statistics* are needed to describe the continuous variables that would be represented in a scatter plot. Correlation means the degree or amount of association or similarity there is between two variables. The correlation coefficient expresses this amount as a number between 0 and 1. The most commonly used procedure produces a correlation coefficient called *r*. If the *r* value is high, for instance 0.8, it means that the two variables are closely related. If the value is low, for instance 0.1, it means that the two variables are not closely related. If the *r* value is negative, for example –0.8, then the two values are negatively related (i.e. the greater the value of one, the lower the value of the other).

For example, in a survey of people's drinking patterns a correlation coefficient of 0.34 (a positive correlation) was calculated between people's normal intake and the amount they drank at Christmas. As one figure increased so did the other. The trend was therefore for the light drinkers to drink lightly at Christmas, and the heavy drinkers to drink heavily at Christmas. In another example, when people were asked how interested they were in exercise a negative correlation was found between the rate of interest and their age, so that the older they were the less interested they were in exercise.

In your reading you may encounter the terms r^2, R and R^2, which are part of regression analysis. Regression is concerned with the nature of the relationship between continuous variables but is a rather advanced statistical procedure for this chapter. Guidance to doing or interpreting these sorts of statistics can be found in Further Reading.

Correlation tests are available for use with either continuous or discrete data. The parametric test is called the Pearson Product–Moment Correlation, the non-parametric test is called the Spearman Rank Order Correlation.

To choose the right test you need first to decide whether parametric or non-parametric measures were used in the data. Parametric means that the data must conform to *parameters* or rules for use with particular tests, such as type of measurement, normally distributed data, random sampling and the same standard deviations for the samples being compared. If in doubt use the non-parametric test: it is less powerful and more cautious than the parametric test. You are more likely to get non-significant results, but if you do show significance then you probably have a real result.

The same rules apply when you are choosing a statistical test to check the results of an experiment for significance. The various inferential tests have been developed to try to assess the difference between experimental groups and conditions, to see whether the independent variable has an effect as hypothesised.

If two different groups or approaches are being compared under the same conditions, like our washing-up liquid experiment in Chapter 6, then the *t*-test (independent samples) is the appropriate parametric test while the Mann-Whitney *U* test is the one for non-parametric data.

If you are comparing the same group of people or matched groups under one or more conditions, as in the example of comparing different teaching methods in Chapter 6, the parametric test is the Matched Pairs *t*-test, and the non-parametric test is the Wilcoxon Matched Pairs Signed Rank Test.

You will find more details about these and other tests in the publications listed under Further Reading on page 137.

COMPUTERS

We have hinted several times at the tremendous advantages of using a computer package to help with your statistics, and strongly recommend that you seek advice on this. Don't be daunted by the technology because the computer can do your calculations in a fraction of the time it would take by hand or by calculator. It is not necessary for you to learn how computers work or to learn computer programming or languages. You only have to learn how to use one of the ready-made statistical packages available.

The Statistical Package for the Social Sciences (SPSS) and Minitab are very powerful statistical packages for large computers, usually available via major educational institutions, some health authorities and local council offices. You will need some training and support to use them.

Increasingly easy-to-use packages are now becoming available for the small personal and desk-top computers, however, and some of them are almost as sophisticated as SPSS and Minitab. They have the added advantage of often being easier to understand and use.

So far we have stressed the advantages of computers. It is only fair to list some of the problems. These are:

- Difficulties in gaining access to a computer.
- The cost of buying your own personal computer.
- The jargon of the programs to be used.
- The frustration when things go wrong.

We have talked of the 'dark days' in research. One of the darkest days must be the one when you have spent the whole day on the computer with your data only to lose it all because of a fault in the system or human error. The comfort to be drawn from such experiences is that you learn so much by your mistakes!

Exercises

All answers are given at the end of the chapter.

Try summarising some data collected in a survey of perceptions of health. Respondents were asked:

'Do you think you should make any changes in your lifestyle to benefit your health?' (Yes/No)

Of the total, 177 said 'Yes' and 70 said 'No'.

1. Express these results in percentages.
   Of those who felt they should make changes in life-style, the following were the responses to the question 'What area of life do you consider a priority for change?' Fifty-four answered 'exercise', 28 'relaxation', 61 said 'diet', 24 'give up smoking' and 10 'cut down on alcohol'.
2. Construct a frequency table, including percentages, for the data.
3. Draw a pie chart of the data in the frequency table you have drawn.
4. Would you express the averages of the perceptions of health data as a mode, median or mean?
5. Try a contingency table on your own bedtime data. As well as age groups you could compare men and women, see if there was a difference in bedtime or hours of sleep between weekends and weekdays, or use any other interesting variables.
6. Try a scatter plot on your own bedtime data. Have you enough observations and a wide enough age range to see a definite pattern?

SCENARIO

Three of the nurses on Ward 4 have generated data for analysis from a number of individual projects relating to the change to becoming a 5-day and day surgery ward.

Sister Jones has been looking at admission lists for surgery to calculate the likely effect on Ward 4 of the change in policy to short-stay. She had also offered to gather data on referrals for Sister Brown.

Sister Brown, the community nurse, has collected data over 2 months on the time spent by community nurses with surgical patients. Later on she will have to process the results of her main survey on how patients and carers cope at home.

Staff Nurse Baker has been comparing the number of times two different types of nursing process notes were used on the ward.

We are not going to discuss all of the results, but we can use some of them for more exercises.

7. Table 9.6 is a table that Sister Jones has compiled to show the surgical admission lists for the hospital over 4 weeks. She is interested in three groups of patients:

Table 9.6 Surgical admission lists for hospital over 4 weeks

| Length of stay | Number of operations per surgeon (A–E) per week | | | | |
	A	B	C	D	E
Week beginning 20 March					
1–2 days	5	1	3	6	7
3–5 days	10	6	10	2	6
6+ days	2	1	4	1	3
Week beginning 27 March					
1–2 days	1	5	7	5	5
3–5 days	4	2	8	5	11
6+ days	0	0	4	0	1
Week beginning 3 April					
1–2 days	2	4	3		6
3–5 days	7	6	12		6
6+ days	2	0	1		1
Week beginning 10 April					
1–2 days		3	6		6
3–5 days		3	8		11
6+ days		0	1		0

- Those staying for 1 or 2 days, because this is the group that might in future be treated as day surgery patients.
- Patients staying between 3 and 5 days. If this group are to be treated as 5-day patients in future then there will be implications for admission. Patients could only be admitted for 5-day stay at the beginning of the week. Admissions later in the week would have to be to another type of ward.
- Long-stay patients, that is patients staying more than 6 days, would also have to be allocated to a different ward or be considered for a 5-day stay. The issue here is that patients would have to be screened carefully for fitness for short-stay surgery, otherwise the workload for the community nurse would be greatly increased.

From Table 9.6 calculate the percentages of patients in each group over the 4-week period.

8. Sister Jones's table of surgical patients referred to the community by hospital liaison sisters over 2 months is shown in Table 9.7. Try converting the table into a histogram, to show the different proportions of surgical patients from each ward over the 2-month period. What proportion of surgical patients are from Ward 4?

Table 9.7 Surgical patients referred to the community over 2 months

Ward	March	April
1	3	1
2	11	12
3	17	15
4	10	11
5	2	2
Total	43	41

9. Table 9.8 shows the data of visiting times to surgical patients collected for Sister Brown by community nurses. If you remember from Chapter 7, the data were recorded over 2 months on the forms shown in Figures 7.21 and 7.22. Fill in the final blank column by calculating the mean time for visits per patient. How would you interpret these results?

10. For her study on the use of the new nursing process notes compared with the existing notes, Staff Nurse Baker developed a checklist of criteria to check whether the different stages of planning had been completed satisfactorily. She found that all 30 patients admitted to her experimental group had full and comprehensive care plans.

In the control group, where the existing notes had been continued, less than 50% of the 30 patients had complete care plans. Although the care given was well documented the stages of assessment, planning and evaluation were often partial and inadequate.

Staff Nurse Baker wants to use a test to see if there is a statistically significant difference between the two groups. Which statistical test would be appropriate?

Table 9.8 Visiting times of community nurses to surgical patients

Ward	No. of patients	%	Average age of patients	Actual time all patients	Average time per patient
1	24	28	44	47h 15m	
2	30	36	49	26h 15m	
3	21	25	44	26h 15m	
4	4	5	64	43h 15m	
5	5	6	45	13h 00m	
Total	84	100	46	156h 00m	

REFERENCE

Guide to Official Statistics (periodic). Central Statistical Office, Cardiff Road, Newport, Gwent.

FURTHER READING

Cormack D F S (ed.) (1984) *The Research Process in Nursing*, chs 14, 15 and 16. Oxford: Blackwell.

Huff D (1973) *How to Lie with Statistics*. Harmondsworth: Penguin Books.

Oldham J (1993) Statistical Tests (Part 1): Descriptive statistics. *Nursing Standard,* **7** (43): 30–35.

Oldham J (1993) Statistical Tests (Part 2): Parametric tests. *Nursing Standard,* **7** (44): 28–30.

Oldham J (1993) Statistical Tests (Part 3): Non-parametric tests. *Nursing Standard,* **7** (45): 28–30.

Polit D and Hungler B (1983) *Nursing Research: Principles and Methods*, chs 14, 15, 16 and 17. Philadelphia: J B Lippincott.

Robson C (1983) *Experiment, Design and Statistics in Psychology,* 2nd edn. Harmondsworth: Penguin Books.

Rowntree D (1981) *Statistics Without Tears*. Harmondsworth: Penguin Books.

Treece E W and Treece J W (1977) *Elements of Research in Nursing*. New York: Mosby.

Waltz C F, Strickland Ora L and Lenz E R (1991) *Measurement in Nursing Research,* 2nd edn. Philadelphia: F A Davis.

ANSWERS TO EXERCISES

1. Of the sample, 77% said Yes, 28% said No (to calculate the percentage each figure was divided by the total of 246 and multiplied by 100).

2. Table of priority areas given by respondents for change in lifestyle

Area of change	*n*	%
Diet	61	35
Exercise	54	30
Relaxation	28	16
Smoking	24	13
Alcohol	10	6
Total	177	100

3. Pie chart of priority areas for change in lifestyle.

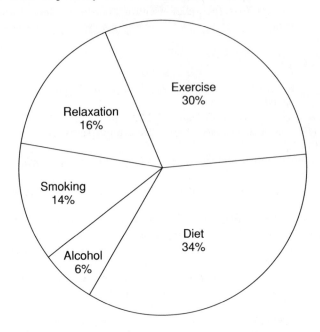

4. Once again, with this type of discrete data the mode is the common-sense choice, because one would want to say that on average more people mentioned diet as priority for change in lifestyle.

7. There is a total of 213 patients over the 4 weeks. Each group expressed as a percentage of that is:

	n	%
1–2 day patients	75	35
3–5 day patients	117	55
6+ day patients	21	10

8. To design the histogram you need, first, to total the figures for 2 months for each ward then convert these to percentages. The table with converted figures would look like:

Table to show hospital liaison referrals for
surgical patients March/April

Ward	No.	%
1	4	5
2	23	27
3	32	38
4	21	25
5	4	5
Total	84	100

From this it can be seen that 25% of surgical patients are from Ward
4. The pattern is clearer still in the histogram.

9. To calculate the mean time for visits per patient convert the actual
   time for each ward into minutes. For example:

   Ward 1: $(47 \times 60) + 15 = 2835$ minutes.

   Then divide the figure by the number of patients:

   $2835 \div 24 = 118$ minutes (rounded figure) = 1 hour 58 minutes.

   There are some interesting differences here. The most striking is
   an average time of 10 hours 49 minutes per patient for surgical
   patients from Ward 4. The column for average age of patients seems
   to give a clue. In fact, Sister Brown discovered that the figures for
   Ward 4 were distorted by one patient who was aged 93 years, taking
   30 hours of day nurse time, and 10 hours of night nurse time.
   Although it was the patient's wish to be at home, Sister Brown ques-
   tioned the disproportionate amounts of community nurse time
   involved. The figures are also an indication of the wide variation in
   community nurse input which would be influenced by changes in
   surgical policy.

   The findings do not really relate to age but to dependence. Sister
   Brown had assumed that there would be a relationship between age
   and time taken but various statistical tests produced no significant
   results.

   There is a variation in average time per patient between all the
   wards. Sister Brown concluded that these needed explaining by
   further investigation of medical records. It could be that different
   wards had different admission policies, or dealt with different kinds
   of surgery.

10. The choice of test would, of course, depend on the type of measure
    Staff Nurse Baker used. It is likely that the measures would be

discrete – for example, simple Yes/No categories or a checklist of criteria for the completion of stages in the nursing process. If she scored each stage on a rating scale of 1–5, however, then the data might be treated as continuous. Generally speaking it would be safer if she chose a non-parametric test. Since she is comparing matched paired groups under two different conditions (the use of new notes compared with existing notes) the correct non-parametric test is the Wilcoxon Signed Rank Test.

10

Ethical Issues in Research

The terms 'ethics' and 'ethical' are used quite frequently in nursing and health care, but just what do they mean? While their actual interpretation and application will differ from person to person there are likely to be common features. *The Concise Oxford Dictionary* (1976) defines ethics as:

'Relating to morals, treating of moral questions, morally correct, honourable'

Cassell's English Dictionary (1966) says:

'Treating of or relating to morals, dealing with moral questions or theory, conforming to a recognised standard'

How we interpret the concept of moral values will be dependent on the society in which we live. In western societies cultural mores determine the rights of the individual. The way these are respected is fundamental to the way the wider community can be judged.

In looking at the way this philosophy relates to nursing research the first question to ask must surely be 'Who constitutes the community?' You might try discussing this in class or with colleagues to find out how different people interpret the concept of 'community'.

For the purposes of this chapter let us consider three constituents:

the researcher,
the respondents and
societal context.

It is all too easy to see each of these elements as having separate ethical needs. However, a little thought will reveal that this is not the case. A nurse may be a researcher in one situation, but a respondent in another and nurses are themselves members of society.

The rights and wrongs and moral duties and obligations then are common to all. It is the perspective by which these terms apply that changes according to the role of the individual in the research context.

Rights and wrongs, duties and obligations in any society must be based on the values of that society. In western civilisation these values tend to concentrate on the individual, and his right to be treated as of worth. No doubt we will each have values that others would not share, but those most likely to be held in common will emphasise this aspect of respect for individuality. How can this be applied to research in general and nursing research in particular?

THE RIGHTS OF INDIVIDUALS

1. Not to be harmed.
2. To self-determination.
3. Of privacy.
4. To confidentiality.
5. To self-respect and dignity.
6. To be able to refuse to participate at any stage of research.
7. Not to be refused services.

We can look at each of these in turn to see just what they mean.

Not to be harmed

This encompasses all forms of distress; physical, psychological and emotional. It is fairly straightforward to see how physical distress might be caused by some forms of research, but less obvious as regards psychological or emotional trauma. Just think, however, about the way respondents chosen because they had cared for a terminally ill relative at home might feel if asked how they felt about the experience, or what were the worst aspects. Distress could also be caused if respondents were asked to face feelings or attitudes, perhaps about themselves, which they prefer to ignore.

To self-determination

Self-determination is more complicated than it appears at first glance. What it means in practical terms is that respondents should only give 'informed consent' to participate; but how can you tell them everything about the research if this may well influence the results? The answer is that information given should be as honest and accurate as possible, but if it is not possible to reveal the true purpose of the research then it is best to state this, but undertake to explain the full facts after the data have been collected.

Of privacy

Privacy is of particular concern during some forms of data collection, such as observation – is it unethical not to tell people they are being observed, whether directly or by the use of mirrors, cameras or tape recorders?

To confidentiality

The amount of information now kept about each of us by different agencies, much of it on computer, makes this a particularly difficult issue. If you promise confidentiality then you must stick to this. The consequence of this, of course, is that it is impossible to follow up interesting questionnaires or similar research instruments where confidentiality was promised. Some way of compensating for this should have been built into the research design, or recognised and accepted at the outset. Some researchers have cheated by using elaborate techniques such as the positioning of stamps on envelopes or some other mark, but this is unethical.

To self-respect and dignity

Clearly, respondents should not deliberately be made to look foolish. This includes the right not to be deceived.

To be able to refuse to participate at any stage of the research

Consent will naturally be sought before any data collection takes place, but it is very hard on the researcher if respondents say they wish to withdraw once a study has commenced. Nevertheless, it must be made clear that they are at liberty to do this.

Not to be refused services

Services such as treatment or health care should not be dependent on agreement to participate. Such conditions constitute pressure, so consent has not been freely given.

VULNERABLE SUBJECTS

There are some groups of people who are not always able to stand up for their own rights; this has ethical implications when the research is concerned with such groups, or where the sample may include these people. Write down the people you feel could be classed as 'vulnerable' in this sense.

You will probably include the following in your list:

Children.
Mentally ill or mentally handicapped.
Aged.
Captive people.
Dying, sedated, or unconscious people.
The very poor, who may be dependent on certain services.

The consent of parents, guardians or other legally responsible people should be sought for the participation of those not capable of making their own decisions. The degree of freedom of captive people and perhaps those in the Armed Forces to refuse participation is debatable. Even where consent is given for or by any of these vulnerable subjects the researcher is still ethically bound not to take undue advantage and abuse their rights.

The whole question of ethics in nursing research was considered so important that in 1977 the Royal College of Nursing issued guidelines for nurses undertaking or associated with research. These guidelines cover nurses undertaking research, nurses in positions of authority where research is carried out and nurses practising in places where research is being carried out. As a profession, nursing must adhere to ethical principles in relation to research and to be seen to do so. As a discipline relatively new to research, nursing must demonstrate that its cherished role as a caring profession does not stop short as soon as it enters a field where issues are far less sharply defined and where the temptations to expediency are great.

THE ROLE OF ETHICAL COMMITTEES

In order to oversee the ethical issues in research in health care, every health district has an ethical committee. Universities and other institutions also have ethical committees. Their actual constitution and terms of reference may differ from place to place, but the principles will be the same. The role of health district committees is to ensure that the research conducted within that district does adhere to an ethical code. Every research project which involves patients in any way should be submitted to the committee for approval prior to its commencement. Just what constitutes a research project is not always clear cut, but any investigation on humans raises ethical issues, whether it is *invasive* (doing something to respondents) or *non-invasive* (use of case records, etc.). Research can also be classified as *therapeutic*, which may benefit the respondent or *non-therapeutic*, which is unlikely to benefit the respondent directly. Both have ethical implications.

As the vast majority of research coming before such committees is of a medical nature – drug trials or new forms of treatment – the emphasis tends to be on medical research. However, the obligation to gain consent for research applies equally to nurses and other health-care workers and an increasing number of the projects being submitted for approval to health district ethical committees nowadays concern research from disciplines other than medicine.

The membership of such committees will differ from district to district, but a typical health district ethical committee will probably consist of approximately three members of the medical staff of consultant status, a general practitioner, a member of the community health council, a member of the health authority and a senior nurse. There may also be someone from the legal profession. If the health district is one which has a university in the area that has some association with health-care teaching or research then there will probably be at least one member from the relevant university faculty.

Ethical committees within other organisations will obviously have a role that reflects the needs of that particular institution and the membership will be selected accordingly. Although the specific roles may differ, all ethical committees serve much the same function and operate on similar principles. It is not, strictly speaking, the responsibility of most ethical committees to decide upon the scientific merit of the subject, design or implementation of the studies brought before it. However, it would clearly be unethical for a committee to give approval to research over which members had serious reservations and various arrangements are made to cope with this eventuality.

Submission to an ethical committee has to be on a formal protocol document, several copies usually being required. Every ethical committee will have its own protocol, but as most of the applications are to do with research from a medical or scientific discipline the protocol is likely to be very detailed and heavily scientifically orientated. This can make it rather difficult for nurses undertaking research to complete. It is a good idea to seek the advice of a nurse who you know has made an application to such a committee, or to seek the help of the secretary of the ethical committee to whom you are making your application.

Whatever the actual format, the protocol will ask certain questions:

- *Researcher's name and appointment*
- *Title of project*
- *Objective (or hypothesis)*
- *The benefits you expect to result from the project*
- *Study design*

    A brief description of what the researcher intends to do, e.g. administer a questionnaire to patients attending out-patients' departments. A copy of any research tools should be attached to the protocol.

- *Scientific background*

For nurse researchers this is likely to be a very brief outline from the literature, e.g. 'Jonson (1984) demonstrated that patients made a satisfactory recovery following herniorrhaphy performed as day-surgery. Madlow (1985) found community nurses expressed positive attitudes towards caring for patients who had undergone day surgery. No work to date has examined the type or duration of care required by such patients following discharge, or their attitude towards this approach to surgery.'

- *Whether the investigation has been done before, i.e. by others*
  It could be a replication, which is acceptable, or that you are conducting the research in a different setting, or using a different sample, or some other modification.
- *If so, why do you wish to repeat it?*
  This is not a problem as long as you are clear about this.
- *How many subjects you will require*
  That is, how big is your sample?
- *Whether this size sample is statistically viable*
  If your research is of a statistical nature then you would need to state the statistical advice you had received.
- *How you intend to select them*
  There must be a rationale for the selection. Opportunism will not do.
- *Whether the use of an animal model has been considered*
  This is not usually applicable to nursing research.
- *Invasive procedures to be carried out on patients*
  This is usually not applicable to nursing research.
- *Samples required*
  This refers to blood, urine or other biological material and is usually non-applicable.
- *How you will go about data collection*
  For example, 'patients will be given a letter at the first post-operative visit explaining the project and asking for their participation. If they agree, a questionnaire will be administered at that and the subsequent three visits by the community nurse. Approximately 20 minutes will be required for completion on each occasion'.
- *Discomfort likely to be experienced by subjects*
  This may seem to be another non-applicable question, but consider the psychological effects your research may have.
- *Hazards or harm to subjects*
  The same considerations as above apply.
- *The precise information to be given to subjects*
  Either the letter of explanation should be quoted or a copy attached to the protocol.

Ethical committees may meet monthly or every 2 months. The application for ethical approval is therefore a vital factor in any research timetable, as data collection cannot proceed without it. Not getting an application in on time could result in a delay of 3 months before the project can continue, so it is worth finding out about this well in advance of the date you wish to start collecting data.

SCENARIO

Ethical consent

Some of the research planned for the evaluation of Ward 4's change to a day- and 5-day ward will require the approval of the district ethical committee.

As a variety of research methods are planned it might be helpful to discuss the proposed research with the ethical committee's secretary or administrator. The phase of the research concerned with examining past records and hospital statistics will not need the committee's consent as it is non-invasive. There would, of course, be considerations of confidentiality to remember if it were intended to look at patients' case notes. Ethical consent is not required, either, for the experimental research on nursing records as this would be regarded as an internal matter which would not directly affect patients in the data collection. On the other hand, the questionnaire to patients and their relatives will require approval from the ethical committee, as will the closed participant observation, directed at the feelings patients express with regard to discharge following surgery. Although this is a non-invasive technique and patients will not be overtly affected in any way, it must be borne in mind that there is a duty to respect any confidential matters heard and be careful to ensure that any research records are kept in a safe and secure place.

There are two other aspects to this question of ethics to remember. First, there is a duty to seek the permission of the relevant manager to carry out any research in a work situation. It is the manager after all who will be ultimately accountable should there be a complaint or some similar difficulty. Secondly, although we have been considering the conduct of nursing research, the medical consultant has responsibility for patients. Discussion with the relevant consultants is not only a matter of courtesy, but their agreement is vital if the research is to succeed.

Exercise

Write down the questions you would want to ask if you were approached for your consent for your 9-year-old child to take part in research into children's attitudes to violence.

Group exercise

Organise a role play in which one member of the class acts as a researcher trying to gain the consent of a group of ward nurses on whom it is intended to conduct non-participant observation of the nature of the nurse–patient interaction, without disclosing the subject of the research.

REFERENCES

Cassell's English Dictionary (1966) London: Cassell.
Concise Oxford Dictionary (1976) Oxford: Oxford University Press.

FURTHER READING

Ashworth P (1984) Accounting for ethics. *Nursing Mirror*, **158**(10): 34–36.
Bulmer M (ed.) (1979) *Censuses, Surveys and Privacy*. London: Macmillan.
Bulmer M (ed.) (1982) *Social Research Ethics: an Examination of the Merits of Covert Participant Observation*. London: Macmillan.
Diers D (1979) *Research in Nursing Practice*, ch. 12. Philadelphia, New York, Toronto: J B Lippincott.
Macleod Clark J and Hockey L (1979) *Research for Nursing: a Guide for the Enquiring Nurse*, pp. 6–11. London: HM and M Publishers.
MacMillan M (1981) A view of ethics. *Nursing Times*, **77**(18): 786–787.
Royal College of Nursing (1977) *Ethics Related to Research in Nursing*. London: Royal College of Nursing.
Royal College of Physicians (1984) *Guidelines on the Practice of Ethical Committees in Medical Research*. London: Royal College of Physicians.
Royal College of Physicians (1990) *Research Involving Patients*. London: Royal College of Physicians.
University College Hospital Ethical Committee (1981) Experience at a clinical research ethical review committee. *British Medical Journal*, **283** (6302): 1312–1314.
Verhonick P J and Seaman C S (1982) *Research Methods for Undergraduate Students in Nursing*, ch. 5. New York: Appleton-Century-Crofts.

11

Communicating Results

TYPE OF REPORT

As we said right at the beginning of this book one of the problems with much nursing research is the difficulty of communicating the results of studies to the rest of the profession. This is in part because not all nurses make the effort to read research articles or reports.

Nevertheless, only by writing up and publishing their studies can nurses who conduct research add to the body of knowledge in nursing. It could be argued that they have a positive duty to do this and so hopefully stimulate debate upon the subject from others. This does, of course, mean that one's work is open to comment and criticism, but this is surely what must happen if nursing is truly to become a research-based profession.

Professional development is, however, only one of the reasons for writing reports and publishing articles. The other reasons which may or may not be applicable in any given situation are as follows;

Reporting back to the funding body

If the research has been funded in any formal way, then most organisations will request a report at the end of the study. Even if they do not it is only courtesy to provide some feed-back so that the organisation can see how their money was spent, the findings which emerged and what benefits may have come about.

Request for further funding

On long-term research a report may be requested at the 'half way' stage and the continued funding may be dependent on the results so far. Alternatively, if the research has been successfully completed but further research is indicated, then a good report can help either in approaching the original funding body or in seeking the support elsewhere.

Informing colleagues

Research is a disturbing and challenging affair and not only to the researcher. Colleagues may well have had to cover some duties, swap days off or take messages for the researcher. Whatever the circumstances no research takes place in a vacuum and colleagues will inevitably have been affected in some way. Informing them just what it was you have been doing all this time and what it is you have found out is not only a courtesy, but also shows them that their co-operation was valuable and worthwhile. If the research was conducted in the work-place, then clearly they need to know about the findings and the implications for practice.

Providing feed-back to participants

Participants may, of course, have been colleagues. However, they might be people you do not expect to be in contact with again. For some a full-scale report would be unsuitable, but you do have a duty to inform those who have agreed to take part in a research study of what was found. Quite what form this takes will depend on the situation, but to ignore the need is arguably unethical.

HOW TO GO ABOUT IT

Inevitably some people are more gifted than others in writing research reports or articles fluently and clearly, but the task can be made simpler by following the basic rules and working through them systematically. In fact, that is the key to successful writing: simply follow the steps of the research process and even if your style lacks polish the report or article will be effective and readable.

One important thing to remember is that how and what you write will depend on the intended audience. The kind of report that would be prepared for a funding organisation would not be appropriate, for example, for colleagues on a ward, or for a journal. It will be different again for participants. However, the same areas need to be covered. What needs to be conveyed is:

Why the study was conducted.
How the study related to previous work in this field.
How it was done.
What were the results.
Where do you go from here.

These points form the sections into which a report is conventionally divided. To put this more formally, the report should contain an introduction, a review of relevant literature, an explanation of the methodology, explanation of the results and finally a section discussing the results, the conclusions and implications of the findings.

Actually getting started on writing the report can be fairly daunting. There are four stages to writing a report:

1. *Preparation*

   This is when you think through the purpose of the report, identify the audience who will read it, checking for accuracy and collecting facts and ideas from different sources. You should start to make notes under the subheadings of the report.

2. *Arrangement*

   What sequence is the convention for your particular field? Select a title that is informative but not verbose. Select the information you will use, being ruthless about rejecting irrelevant material. Then revise and decide on the order. Separate files or a card index may help. Put the material under the headings you have chosen, adding extra notes as required. Decide whether there will be appendices, illustrations and so on and how you are going to arrange these.

3. *Writing*

   Write clearly and simply. Using flowery language or jargon will not make your report seem more learned, in fact quite the reverse. The purpose after all is to communicate.

4. *Revising*

   Give yourself time for this. It is a good idea to put the draft to one side for a few days then go back to it again. Make sure the pages are numbered correctly, that diagrams and appendices are labelled and that references are complete and accurate. Asking someone else to read it through can be helpful.

So just what should go in each section? Although the actual contents will vary according to the particular circumstances, below is a guide to the things you need to take into account.

INTRODUCTION

A report or paper has to be written as if those who read it will know little or nothing of the subject. Of course, this is rarely the case in practice but the point is that you must not assume that people will automatically know what you mean unless you tell them. The introduction has to set the scene, as it were, explaining how the research came about, in what way you were involved in that field and the importance of the research with regard to current practice. Why is it of interest to you, or anyone else? The introduction has to explain the context of the research and to convince the reader that it is worthwhile reading on.

LITERATURE REVIEW

The nature of the literature review will depend in part on the audience for which you are writing. If the paper is an internal report or to a funding body, then it might not be appropriate to give an extensive review of the literature unless you are requested to do so. Nevertheless, some discussion of previous work on the subject and the different theories which form part of current thinking on the subject is necessary if your paper is not to appear trivial and lacking in depth. You will need to be rigorous in deciding just what literature is central to an understanding of the subject. This is a very good discipline in writing pithy but useful reports!

On the other hand, should the paper be intended for publication or be part of the requirements for a course of some kind, then the literature review could well take up a quarter to a third of the entire paper. This is because you will need to provide a much fuller discussion concerning previous work, the varying theories that may have been argued and the literature which led you to the formulation of your hypothesis and theoretical framework. This is not simply writing for the sake of it – if you wish to persuade the readers that your research has been meaningful, then you must demonstrate that your work has been conducted in the light of, not in ignorance about, other research on this topic.

METHODOLOGY

It is important to explain precisely how you went about the study and what form your data collection took. The things to include in this section are:

1. What method of data collection was used, a questionnaire, observation, interviews or whatever. If you are writing for publication, then it is not feasible to give the whole of your research instrument – the complete interview schedule for instance, but you can include one or two items as examples. In a full report or large-scale piece of research it is the convention to give the whole of the instrument in the form of an appendix at the end.

2. Why you chose this method instead of others. As we said in the chapter on research design there is no 'right way' to conduct research, so you need to explain the thinking behind the method you adopted. What led you to reject alternative approaches? What were the advantages and disadvantages of the methods you rejected and, just as important, what were the advantages and disadvantages of what you did do? What problems were encountered in the research, and how were these overcome? Would you do the research in the same way with the benefit of hindsight?

3. How the sample for research was chosen, how respondents were contacted and their consent obtained. If there are ethical implica-

tions or difficulties these should be discussed and the decisions made justified.

4. The arrangements made for the analysis, whether this was manual or by computer. The results themselves come in the next section, but you should explain how the analysis was carried out and if help was given by anyone else. If, for example, a statistician actually put the data onto a computer and ran the analysis for you, or assisted you in doing it yourself, then you should state this.

RESULTS

It is easier for others to read if results are presented separately from the discussion about their interpretation, but it may not be easy to do this in a limited space. However, try to avoid a jumble of tables, graphs, lists of numbers and so on mixed up with the text on what they mean. The chapter on data analysis will have given you some ideas on how to present data in a clear and methodical manner. One graph can be worth a hundred words, so think who your readers will be and whether they will be able to understand what you are showing them. Obviously, only the most important results can be presented in an article where the number of words is limited, but other papers should contain all your findings. Again, if these are extensive then some could be put in an appendix.

DISCUSSION, CONCLUSION AND IMPLICATIONS

Having presented your results you should discuss just what they mean. It's all very well to state that in answer to question 14 which was about pre-operative anxiety, 20% of patients answered 'very', 60% answered 'quite' and 20% said 'not at all', but what does that mean for practice in surgical nursing and how does it relate to the question about previous admission to hospital for example? More importantly, what are the implications for practice in the future?

The recommendations you may wish to make concerning change should follow logically from the discussion, supported as that is by the results. It is often said that all research does is come up with more questions, but that should not be regarded as a criticism. Once you begin to investigate an issue you are more than likely to discover that there is more to it than you first thought and further research is necessary. It would be a sterile piece of work which led nowhere!

PRESENTATION

What should this report look like? For a start it should be attractive. That does not mean that it has to be on glossy paper but it should be neat and tidy. Hand-written reports or articles are not acceptable, but the advent of word processors means that it is easier these days to get your work in typed format, or you could get someone to type it for you. A report, such as you would write for a sponsoring body should have the following:

Title page

This should include the name of the author and the date.

Acknowledgements

You will have been helped on your way by numerous people, and it is only courteous that you should thank them in a public manner. You don't need to name them all individually, but something like:

'My thanks to the Friends of St Agnes' Hospital who funded this work, to the computer section at Hightown College of Further Education who gave valuable advice on the analysis, and not least to my colleagues in Ward 4 for their support and encouragement.'

List of contents

This should contain the headings of the various sections and the number of the page on which they start. It makes for easier reading if each section starts on a fresh page and each page should be numbered. There should also be a list of Tables or Figures, giving the caption of each one and the page number. If you have any appendices these should be listed stating what each is and again, a page number. Conventionally the appendices are given Roman numerals, e.g. 'Questionnaire page ix'. This distinguishes the appendix from the main text.

Summary

The summary should do what the name implies, that is summarise the work. A large report will probably have a summary of 200 words, a more modest piece of work would only require a sentence or two, for example:

'A study was conducted on fifty patients following herniorrhaphy to investigate their experience of community care after discharge. While the majority considered their needs to have been met, a significant number felt they would have benefited from greater involvement with the Community Nursing Sister. Changes in the liaison system following surgery are recommended.'

Chapters or sections

Appendices

List of references

In the text you will only have referred to other work as 'Jones (1)', or 'Jones, 1987'. The references would then be listed in numerical order, or alphabetically:

1. Jones B C (1987) *Nursing for Students*. London: Blackstock Publications.
2. Smith A B (1986) *Community Care*. Manchester: White Publishing.

Make sure your references are complete and correct. If you were careful enough to record them as you went along then you should have no problems, but if not you are in for a frustrating time searching them out again!

Even if your research was small scale, going through the process of preparing a report is a very useful skill to learn. Writing a report will give you the opportunity to reflect on the experience and decide on the next step.

WRITING FOR PUBLICATION

The most important point in getting your work accepted for publication is to submit it to the most appropriate journal in the first place. Consider the topic of the research and ask yourself what kinds of people would be interested in reading about it. It could be suitable for one of the 'popular' nursing journals but if it is very specialised, or for a particular speciality in nursing – community nurses, for instance, then the journal which caters for that particular group of nurses would be best.

Most journals have guidelines for contributors to help in the preparation of articles submitted for publication. If you can't find these in back copies of the journal in question, it is worth writing or telephoning to ask for details to be sent to you. In general, journals will ask for manuscripts to be double-spaced with a margin of 1 to 1½ inches.

You should send the original manuscript, not a photocopy, but remember to keep at least one copy for yourself. Length will vary according to the journal, but 1500 to 2000 words is about right for most publications. You could telephone or write to the most appropriate journal, saying you have an article on so-and-so and would they be interested in publishing it? This will save a great deal of time if they are not publishing the kind of material you are offering, so you can then apply elsewhere.

Much of what has already been said about writing reports also applies to writing for publication, but there are some particular points to bear in mind.

1. The content and style will depend on the intended readership. It is useful to read several copies of the journal to which you intend to submit your work in order to get a 'flavour' of the articles the journal publishes.
2. The title of the paper needs to be particularly clear and concise, and accompanied by a statement of who you are.
3. The literature you discuss and references you give should be those that are most central to the research. References should be presented in the convention adopted by the particular publication to which you intend to submit your article. There simply is not space for everything you read which had some bearing on the topic or the way it was investigated.
4. Only an outline and the purpose of the methodology should be given. Again, detailed explanation is not possible or appropriate.
5. Choose the tables and figures you present with care. Limit these to findings which demonstrate the most crucial results. Remember, some people may only read your work in journal form, so get across the most important points.
6. There should be some discussion of the implications of the results although of necessity not extensive, but it will probably not be appropriate to give recommendations except in general terms, as these are specific to the setting in which the work was conducted.
7. The limitations of the work – what you would do, or not do, again, unexpected difficulties encountered and ways in which the research could have been improved should be stated. This is not just 'washing one's dirty linen in public'! It demonstrates that you are fully aware of any faults and have considered them both for your own benefit and for research on that topic in the future. Besides, it is better to admit one's shortcomings or mistakes than have others point them out later!
8. As with reports, it is usual to acknowledge those who have helped in the research, or gave permission for it to be conducted.

Nurses are often reluctant to write up their work for the nursing press, feeling it is not really sufficiently interesting or substantial to merit publication. Remember, though, that for every established researcher whose papers frequently appear in the journals there was a first time! Even if your paper is rejected the exercise of writing up is a learning experience and you may receive some helpful comments from the editor or referee. You'll find the glow of finally seeing your work in print very satisfying!

Writing a Report

1. In the scenarios and exercises in this book we have used the example of a surgical ward which is to become a day- and 5-day ward to illustrate various research aspects and techniques. From the information given, see if you can write the introduction for a report to be presented to the clinical director.
2. Put yourself in the place of one of the staff mentioned in the scenarios and write the section on research design and methodology for an article to be submitted for publication to one of the nursing journals.
3. Think of a piece of research you would like to do in your own clinical area, then make a list of the journals for which you think an article on this subject would be most appropriate.

FURTHER READING

Burnard P (1992) *Writing for Health Professionals: a Manual for Writers*. London: Chapman & Hall.

Cheadle J (1984) Presenting your research. *Nursing Mirror*, **146**(18): 26–28.

Cormack D F S (with contributions from D C Benton) (1994) *Writing for Health Care Professions*. Oxford: Blackwell Scientific Publications.

Killien M G (1988) Disseminating and using research findings. *Nursing Research, Theory and Practice*, eds Woods N F and Catanzaro M, ch. 31. St Louis: Mosby.

Notter L (1979) The research report: communicating the findings. *Essentials of Research in Nursing*, ch. 10. London: Tavistock.

Polit D and Hungler B (1985) Research reports. *Essentials of Nursing Research*, ch. 19. Philadelphia: J B Lippincott.

Tierney A (1984) Writing and publishing a research report. *The Research Process in Nursing*, ed. Cormack D F S, ch. 17. Oxford: Blackwell Scientific Publications.

Tornquist E M (1986) *From Proposal to Publication: an Informal Guide to Writing About Nursing Research*. Menlo Park, Cardiff: Addison-Wesley.

Treece E W and Treece J W (1986) 'Writing the research report' and 'Publication of the research report'. *Elements of Research in Nursing*, chs. 25 and 26. St Louis: Mosby.

12

Writing a Research Proposal

Writing a research proposal is an essential procedure which can contribute much to the success of any research project. It is not just a requirement for funding applications.

REASONS FOR WRITING A PROPOSAL

What is the purpose of a proposal? Well, the proposal can serve a number of purposes.

First, if the researcher is seeking funding in order to undertake the research, then the proposal is necessary to explain to the body being approached exactly what is intended. The quality of the proposal and the way in which it is prepared will help to demonstrate that the applicant has thought through the research carefully, appears competent to conduct the work and is clear as to what he or she is intending to do.

Secondly, writing the research proposal is an excellent way for the researcher to clarify her thoughts. A proposal is like a blueprint and in preparing it the researcher will have to be specific as to the nature and purpose of the research. Writing the research proposal is the crunch event which turns a collection of woolly ideas and vague hopes into a realistic exposition of intent.

Thirdly, a good proposal serves as a guide in writing the report at the end of the study.

Fourthly, if the researcher is conducting the study as part of the requirements for a degree or some other form of higher education a research proposal may well be required by the department at the university or college with which the researcher intends to register. Indeed, acceptance for registration is usually dependent upon the quality of the research proposal.

The research proposal should cover three things:

1. Why the study should be done.

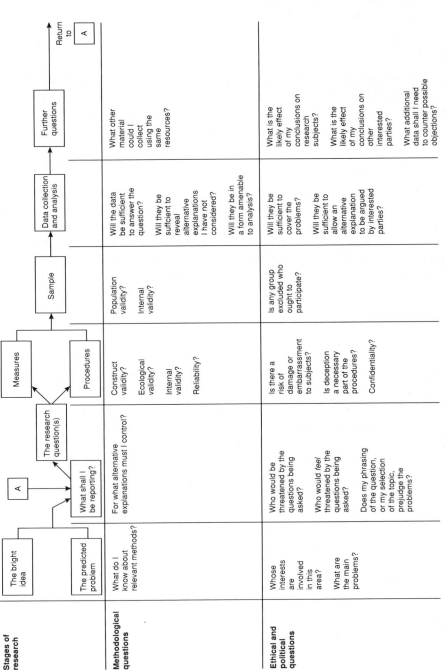

Figure 12.1 Constructing a research proposal (Reproduced with permission from Open University, Course DE304, Research Methods in Education and the Social Sciences)

2. How it is to be conducted.
3. What will be the benefits of completing the study.

STYLE

In most cases when researchers apply for funds the research proposal has to be submitted to the funding body to examine before a decision is made whether or not to even interview the applicant. Therefore it has to speak for her; it has to 'sell' the idea on its merits.

Sometimes a funding body or other organisation may issue guidelines as to how a proposal should be set out. It is a good idea to emphasise those aspects of the research which you consider will be of particular relevance to that specific organisation. Although the research will probably have been discussed with a lecturer if further education is involved, the same considerations apply. It goes without saying that the proposal must be convincing. If it reads as being rather vague, then those reading it will question whether the researcher is really competent and committed.

Equally obviously it should look good. A neat, well-organised, clear proposal will carry far more weight than a bundle of dog-eared papers that are hard to read and understand.

STEPS FOR PREPARATION

It is worth following the steps listed below before you actually complete the proposal. This will help to ensure that all the major aspects have been covered.

1. Write down the study objective and research questions to achieve that objective as clearly as possible. Do not try to put the world to rights in one go! You will only end up with confused objectives and numerous overlapping questions.
2. Review the literature. This will of course be part of the research process, but demonstrating a knowledge of previous work in the subject and how your proposal relates to this will show that you have given the matter some thought.
3. Plan your overall design. Decide whether the approach is to be (survey, interpretative or experimental). The objectives of the study will probably indicate the most appropriate design. Then you can work on developing the research tools.
4. Decide to which funding agency or research body application will be made. Some may have their own proposal protocols, so the proposal will need to be prepared in the required format. Funding agencies and funding are discussed in Chapter 14.
5. Seek a 'mentor'. If this is your first attempt at research, the advice

and support of someone more experienced will be invaluable and save many pitfalls. Even experienced researchers discuss their plans with colleagues, so don't feel embarrassed about seeking help. Find out if the health district or trust has a research adviser, or if there is a research interest group. The Royal College of Nursing has a full-time research adviser who can probably provide a local contact for you.

6. Think through what it is you hope the eventual analysis will look like. With quantitative data, the tables, charts and so on that may result are fairly easy to visualise, but it is more difficult to speculate upon qualitative data. The point of the exercise is that it will shed some light on the quality of the data you can expect to collect and therefore whether it will prove worthwhile.

7. Be brief but clear. Funding bodies are not likely to be swayed according to the weight of the documentation before them. Indeed, as they often have many such proposals to read they are likely to be less enthusiastic over considering one of daunting volume.

8. Keep supporting papers brief. Specifically what is included in a proposal in the way of appendices may be laid down by the funding body. If not, ask yourself if the intended appendix is relevant and necessary. If it is not, then leave it out.

9. Realistically assess the required resources. If the intended research will require the use of a computer and you have no access to one, how do you propose to overcome this? How much time will the research really take and will you be able to take this time out from work?

10. Cost the research carefully. Find out how much it will cost to type and photocopy the research tools you plan to use. What will the postage be? What mileage rate is reasonable for travel? It is much better to get this right before you send in a proposal than to run out of money before the research is complete. The funding body will not be too keen to consider a request for further funding if this happens.

CONTENTS OF A PROPOSAL

As previously discussed, some bodies have specially prepared proposal forms and although they will differ from one another they are all likely to include the following.

Title

The research proposal must have a working title, even though it is possible that the emphasis of the research may shift as it proceeds. Try not to make the title too long, though it should make clear what the subject of the research is.

Name of the investigator

This sounds too obvious to need saying, but the point is you need to ensure that your name is clearly written on the document itself, not only on the accompanying letter, which can become separated from the proposal. If the research is a collaborative effort with others, then they too need to be included in the proposal. A more formal proposal may ask you to provide the curriculum vitae of the person or persons applying.

Date of submission

This looks equally obvious, but if the research lasts 2 or 3 years and you were committed to completing it within a certain time scale, there should be a record of precisely when it was started.

Statement of the problem

Here it must be stated clearly what research problem you are studying. The proposal is most likely to succeed if this problem, while specific to the area of your inquiry, has more general application. A research problem that was only of relevance to a particular clinical area and had no application to similar settings is unlikely to gain support. The problem should be of a manageable size, given the resources at your disposal and the time scale envisaged.

The problem can be in the form of an hypothesis, or it can be expressed as a question which the research is intended to answer.

Importance of the problem

Is there really a requirement for research into the problem you have identified? Nowadays, funding bodies tend to target particular subjects on which researchers are invited to submit proposals. This does not necessarily mean that research into other topics will automatically be ruled out, but it does mean that you need to be careful to apply to the appropriate organisation, and be very clear why your research should be given consideration. It may be of interest to you, but is anyone else likely to think the same? Who will benefit from the work? Will there be implications for further research? If there is a theoretical basis for the study, or if it will contribute to previous theory, then this should be discussed. You may consider that the research will contribute new theory to the field of knowledge on the subject, in which case discuss how this might come about. Is the project unique, or has the same or similar work been done before? This would not rule it out as long as you can make a case for repeating it, or demonstrate the singular feature of what is proposed.

Objectives of the study

What is it you are setting out to achieve? The objectives should be realistic, and they should relate to the problem as it has been outlined. The objectives which are stated should be specific and measurable. 'To improve nursing care' will not do!

Precis of the literature

The proposal should contain a résumé of the relevant literature. This should be aimed at presenting an overview of the subject or topic to be studied. Past studies of particular interest and the strengths and weaknesses of these should be discussed, demonstrating how the research being proposed will explore these problems. The literature review might pick upon suggestions or leads for further research suggested by other researchers and present a synopsis of the results of past work. The literature should be as up to date as possible, emphasising current research.

Research design

The proposal should state first what approach it is intended to pursue – historical, experimental, descriptive or case-study. Secondly, the hypothesis to be tested or the research question to be investigated should be clearly set out. Thirdly, the definitions you intend to use, the limitations of the research and the assumptions being made must be clearly set out.

Research implementation

Although at the proposal stage it is not usually expected to include prepared questionnaires or other research tools, you should have some idea as to how the required data will be collected, what kind of data you intend to collect and the facilities necessary for the analysis. This latter point is particularly true if the analysis will be dependent on computer facilities and advice. The approving body will want to be sure that you have made or are making arrangements for this and that the research will not grind to a halt because you overlooked the problem of analysing a large volume of data.

Resources

If the proposal is being written in order to apply for funding for the research, then it must state how much money will be required and how it will be spent. If salary costs for yourself or others are required, even on a part-time basis, then just how much will this be? Travel associated with the research, the cost of printing or photocopying data sheets, questionnaires or other research tools, typing and postage must all be included here. The timetable is another factor, especially where the funding request is of a major nature and includes the salary of the researcher or research team.

Preparing a proposal is, as you can see, a major task but one which cannot be skimped. A poor proposal almost inevitably leads to poor research, even if the work is of a modest nature. Thinking through all the elements of the research in a logical fashion in order to write a proposal is an essential first step in any research undertaking. In the last chapter we will consider some recent developments in the way nursing research is being encouraged, funded and taught.

SCENARIO

A research proposal

Staff Nurse Baker decides to use the change to 5-day surgery on Ward 4 as the research project required for her staff development course. The amount of money being sought is therefore fairly modest, as it is only intended to cover research expenses. The research proposal she finally drafts is shown below:

Implications for nursing practice of 5-day surgery

Susan Baker, Registered General Nurse, Intensive Therapy Certificate. Senior Staff Nurse, Ward 4, St Agnes' Hospital.
12 September 1989.

Background to the study
The increase in day surgery and the utilisation of 5-day wards is a policy which has become increasingly widespread during the last 10 years. It is stated DHSS[1] policy to encourage this form of treatment in order to reduce waiting lists. The costs per patient treated are also less, and there is some evidence that such treatment is more convenient and well accepted by patients.

While such wards have been in operation for some time in this country, the clinical needs of these patients have received little attention (Ruckley[3]).

The Clinical Director for Surgery intends to introduce a day surgery and 5-day ward undertaking minor general surgery in the next financial year. The aim of the research is to:

1. Examine the precise care needs of patients treated on the new ward.
2. Determine the most effective and efficient way of meeting these needs.

The findings would hopefully be of relevance not only to the proposed facility but to similar facilities also.

Literature review

Day surgery is not quite the modern innovation in patient care that it is often assumed to be. Nicoll[3] published the first account of day surgery in 1909, and considered that patients experienced less pain and had a lower incidence of respiratory and circulatory complications. Burn[4] states that as cost per patient is less, more patients can be treated using the same facilities. However, in a survey in 1980 of 30 health districts who had 5-day units, Davies et al.[5] found that 13 of the units were an addition to pre-existing facilities, the aim being to reduce waiting lists.

Burn[4] and Ruckley et al.[6] both suggest that community nursing staff welcomed the variety of patients that day and 5-day surgery brought onto their case load.

Little research so far appears to have approached the question from the point of view of the patient. This study is intended to examine what kind of information would be most appropriate both before and after discharge, and what special care needs these patients have while in hospital.

Research design and method

The research is in two stages.

1. It is intended to visit several hospitals around the country which have day surgery and 5-day units in order to study their policies and procedures.
2. The criteria by which patients will be selected for day care or 5-day surgery have already been established by the surgical division. Using these criteria, patients from the waiting list will be randomly selected to take part in a survey aimed at defining what pre- and post-operative information they consider would be helpful. The project will be explained to them verbally and by a printed description at outpatients clinic. If consent to take part is given, patients will be interviewed at home on an agreed date.

Sample

One hospital from each of six different health regions will be visited for the first part of the research. A sample of 60 patients will be randomly chosen for the survey. This size sample has been chosen so that, assuming a 50% response rate, the sample will still allow some statistical analysis.

Analysis
Data from visits to other hospitals will be examined for examples and indications for good practice. The patient survey will be analysed qualitatively for consistent themes in responses to open-ended questions, and by computer for the demographic and structured questions.

Ethical considerations
Patients will already have been told of the way in which their operation is to be performed (i.e. day or 5-day admission) by their consultant, prior to an approach being made. They will be given time to consider participation. Evidence from similar studies suggests that patients welcome the opportunity to discuss forthcoming treatment with a health care worker. Any difficulties identified will be discussed with the consultant, who has given his support to the study. Measures will be taken to preserve confidentiality of questionnaire responses.

Resources
Hightown College has agreed to undertake the computer analysis of the patient survey results as a student project. The resource requirements therefore do not include the cost of analysis.

Travel

Visits to six hospitals with day or 5-day units	£250
Typing of letters to 60 patients	£50
Typing and photocopying of questionnaires	£100
Postage	£50
Typing and photocopying of report	£50
	£500

References

1. DHSS (1976) *Priorities for Health and Personal Social Services*. London: HMSO.
2. Ruckley C V (1971) Team approach to early discharge and out-patient surgery. *Lancet*, **1**: 177–180.
3. Nicoll J H (1909) The surgery of infancy. *British Medical Journal*, **2**: 753–754.
4. Burn J (1983) Responsible use of resources: day surgery. *British Medical Journal*, **3286**: 492–493.
5. Davies R, Cliff K S and Waters W E (1981) Present use of 5-day wards. *British Medical Journal*, **282**: 2118–2119.
6. Ruckley C V, Ferguson J B D and Cuthbertson C (1981) A 5-day ward as part of a comprehensive surgical service. *British Medical Journal*, **282**: 1525–1528.

FURTHER READING

Brittain R D (1980) Money and methods for research in the National Health Service. *Royal Society of Health Journal*, **100**, (3): 79–81.

Polit D F and Hungler P B (1985) *Essentials of Nursing Research*, pp. 364–365. London: J B Lippincott.

Richards D (1990) Ten steps to successful grant writing. *Journal of Nursing Administration*, **20** (1).

Sleep J (1989) *Writing a Research Proposal and Applying for Funding*. London: Royal College of Midwives.

Treece E W and Treece J W (1986) *Elements of Research in Nursing*, pp. 117–122. St Louis: Mosby.

Woods N F (1988) Generating a research proposal. *Nursing Research, Theory and Practice*, eds Woods N F and Catanzaro M, ch. 32. St Louis: Mosby.

13

Audit and Research

In 1989 the Department of Health issued the White Paper *Working for Patients* (DoH, 1989). This set out proposed changes to the organisation of the NHS which were made law by the 1990 NHS and Community Care Act. One important feature of this was that doctors were, in future, to be required to examine the quality of their clinical practice. Since then, resources have been made available to enable medical staff to audit their work. Although nurses, midwives and other clinical professions were not specifically mentioned in the White Paper, gradually the emphasis has shifted from audit of medical practice to audit of clinical practice – that is, the care given by any and all heath care professionals. In 1993, funds provided to support audit were for all health professionals, not only doctors.

Nurses and midwives, as well as some therapy professionals, have in fact been engaged in auditing or evaluating their care for some years (Gray, 1987). However, as in the medical profession it was somewhat sporadic and usually involved only a few enthusiasts, mostly working in their own time with few resources to help them. Now, all who work in health care are being actively encouraged to audit their professional practice, with funds and training made increasingly available.

It is not the intention of this chapter to give a 'crash course' in clinical audit, nor to go into detail as to the factors and influences which have brought about this change. Many people are very confused, however, as to the relationship between research and audit, so what we will try to do is to clarify the differences, similarities and interactions of the two activities.

DEFINITIONS OF AUDIT

Audit originally meant 'a hearing before peers' (Buckingham, 1975) and the peer review element is very important. The definition of audit given by the DoH (1989) was;

'the systematic, critical analysis of the quality of medical care, including the procedures used for diagnosis and treatment, the use of resources, and the resulting outcome and quality of life for the patient'.

Although this definition is widely quoted, it does leave out the main purpose of audit, which is to identify deficiencies and take steps to remedy them. A definition now in more general use for clinical audit is:

'Clinical audit is the systematic critical analysis of the quality of clinical care, by all those who contribute to care. It includes the procedures used for diagnosis and treatment, the use of resources, and the resulting outcome and quality of life for the patient – for this the patients' views must be sought. Its objectives are improvement in the quality of clinical practice' (Moss, 1992)

SIMILARITIES AND DIFFERENCES

The characteristics common to audit and research are that both must be conducted in a manner which has scientific rigour, is objective and systematic. As with research, audit must be carefully designed and the method of data collection must be decided. Data are then collected and analysed. Finally the results have to be interpreted. However, in audit the next step is to identify whether and what changes to practice or service delivery are necessary, and how to bring these about. Donabedian (1966) distinguished between the assessment of medical technology (research) and the assessment of the quality of medical care (audit). In other words, while research is about finding out what is the best treatment or management, audit asks the question 'are we carrying out what research has demonstrated to be best practice?'

If we take each step in turn, then we can see the role of research at each stage of the cycle.

1. *Identify the topic.* There is no point in conducting audit simply for the sake of it – it must have a purpose. In deciding what topic would be most useful to audit, published research might present findings about practice which set you thinking as to how your clinical area compares. You might wish to introduce a new idea that you have read about, then use audit to see if it produces the intended outcome.
2. *Setting standards.* Whatever the topic, standards need to be set as to the practice you consider you *should* be providing, so that audit can compare what is with what ought to be. Up to date research findings should be the basis for setting these standards.
3. *Measuring practice against standards.* Knowledge of research techniques can be very useful in deciding what data you need to collect and how to collect it. Questionnaires, recording sheets and analysis

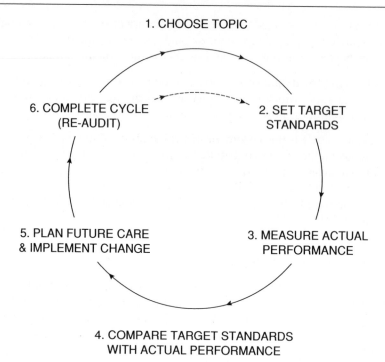

Figure 13.1 The audit cycle

of documents can all be used for audit. As well as this, audit data must be collected in an objective and logical manner, just as research data is.

4. *Analysing data.* Most audit data will be quantitative in nature – that is, consisting of numbers. Methods for handling the raw data are very similar, whether the purpose is research or audit.

5. *Interpreting results.* Once analysed, findings have to be related to the clinical setting and clinical practice. Research can be helpful in making sense of what you have found.

6. *Choosing a course of action.* As in setting standards, what you decide to do to make any improvements indicated by the audit should be based on current knowledge, supported by research findings as to what constitutes best practice.

7. *Implementing change.* Actually bringing about change is much more difficult to do than simply stating what change should happen. Research into how people learn, their attitudes, or how they interact might suggest strategies for bringing about the changes needed to improve care.

What, then, are the differences? Madden (1991) sets them out like this:

Research

- May involve experiments on human subjects.
- Is a systematic investigation which aims to increase the sum of knowledge.
- May involve the administration of a placebo.
- May involve allocating patients randomly to different treatment groups.
- May involve a completely new treatment.
- May involve extra disturbance or work beyond that required for normal clinical management.
- Usually involves an attempt to test a hypothesis.
- May involve the application of strict selection criteria to patients with the same problem before entering them into the research study.

Audit

- Never involves experiments on human subjects.
- Is a systematic approach to the peer review of medical care in order to identify opportunities for improvement and to provide a mechanism for bringing them about.
- Never involves a placebo treatment.
- Never involves allocating patients randomly to different treatment groups.
- Never involves a completely new treatment.
- Never involves disturbance to the patient beyond that required for normal clinical management.
- May involve patients with same problem being given different treatments but only after full discussion of the known advantages and disadvantages of each treatment. The patients are allowed to choose freely which treatment they get.

If there are so many differences what then is the relationship between audit and research? One way to think about this is that research can be both the chicken and the egg as far as audit is concerned.

Audit requires that those undertaking the review know the best way to treat or manage patients. That is why audit has to be a review among peers, as only those who have a knowledge of the clinical condition are in a position to judge whether or not best care is being delivered. However, that judgement must be based on the most up to date information as to what is the best treatment for patients with a particular condition or problem. Current research findings therefore should provide the basis on which the standards against which performance is audited are set.

Once an audit has been carried out the results may indicate that care is not as good as it could or should be. Knowledge of the most recent research can help in deciding what the alternatives are for changing the situation to bring about improvement. If changes are made without evidence that the new form of treatment or management is effective then the care will not be improved. The implications of audit for setting research priorities are categorised by Vuori (1989) as follows:

Concepts related to quality, e.g. accommodating consumer and provider views, the relationship between quality, cost containment and technology.

Epidemiology of quality, e.g. variations in the distribution and quality of care, influences on clinical decision making.

Quality assurance methods, e.g. measurement tools, service provision.

Criteria and standards: developing, testing and costing.

Implementation: how organisations and individuals bring about change.

Organisation: the effect of managerial and care strategies.

Evaluation: the impact on patient care and outcomes of quality assurance.

A knowledge of the research process and research methods can help in conducting audit. Clear objectives need to be set and the variables carefully defined. Literature must be searched to find out whether others have audited the same aspects of care and if so, how it was done. Audit design includes deciding which patients to include, the time period, sampling and data collection methods. Data must be analysed using appropriate and correct techniques. The audit must then be reported without bias and presentation of findings made. Applying research techniques to audit helps to ensure that it is carried out well and the subsequent findings can be confidently regarded as valid.

A further aspect of the relationship between research and audit is that if audit findings demonstrate that the care given was not delivered in line with expectations, or did not have the intended outcome, it may be that research is needed to find out why. The two activities are therefore different, but complementary.

REFERENCES

Buckingham W B (1975) Audit – a definition. *Quarterly Review Bulletin*, **1**(3): 18.
Department of Health (1989) *Working for Patients*, Cmnd. 555. London: HMSO.
Donabedian A (1966) Evaluating the quality of medical care. *Milbank Memorial Fund Quarterly*, **44**: 166–206, Part 2 (July).
Gray A (1987) A mixed review. *Senior Nurse*, **6**(2): 6–8.
Madden A P (1991) Research and audit. *Network*. London: King's Fund Centre.
Moss F (1992) Achieving quality in hospital practice. *Quality in Health Care*, **1** **Supplement:** 17–19.

Vuori H (1989) Research needs in quality assurance. *Quality Assurance in Health Care*, **1**: 147–159.

FURTHER READING

Department of Health (1989) *Working for Patients: Working Paper 6*. London: HMSO.

Department of Health (1991b) *Medical Audit in the Hospital and Community Health Services*, HC(91)2. London: Department of Health.

Department of Health (1991) *Framework of Audit for Nursing Services*. London: Department of Health.

Department of Health (1994) *Evolution of Clinical Audit*. London: Department of Health.

Ellis R and Whittington D (1993) *Quality Assurance in Health Care: a Handbook*. London: Edward Arnold.

Quality in Health Care, **1**, Supplement: S17–S19. Halifax: BMJ Publishing Group.

Russel I T and Wilson B J (1992) Audit: the third clinical science. *Quality in Health Care*, **1**(1): 51–55. Halifax: BMJ Publishing Group.

Samuel O, Lackin P and Sibbald B (1993) *Counting on Quality. A Medical Audit Workbook*. Exeter: Royal College of General Practitioners.

Shaw C D (1990) Aspects of audit: the background. *British Medical Journal*, **i**: 1256–1258.

Shaw C D (1990) Aspects of audit: acceptability of audit. *British Medical Journal*, **i**: 1443–1446.

Shaw C D (1992) *Specialty Medical Audit*. London: King's Fund Centre.

Walshe K and Coles J (1993) *Evaluating Audit. Developing a Framework*. London: CASPE Research.

Wright C C (1992) *Quality Assurance: an Introduction for Health Care Professionals*. Edinburgh: Churchill Livingstone.

14

The Future for Nursing Research

The main purpose of this book is to unravel the mystique that is attached to the concept of research. For many this may well be enough, but some of you may wish to carry your interest further.

In the past nursing research has been organised and funded in a some-what piecemeal fashion. Although Nursing Research Units have been set up, such as those at King's College, University of London and the Nursing Practice Unit at the University of Surrey, most nursing research has been conducted by nurses working largely in isolation, or with a few like-minded individuals. Funding for nursing research has been similarly uncoordinated, with those who were keen to carry out research having to apply to wher-ever or whoever they felt might be supportive. Now, however, significant new developments with regard to the way health-care research is organ-ised, funded and implemented, together with changes to the training of nurses, have significantly changed this and presented nurses with new and interesting opportunities.

RESEARCH AND DEVELOPMENT IN THE NHS

In 1990 the post of National Director of Research and Development was created by the Secretary of State for Health. The role of the Director is to coordinate the efforts of all the various bodies engaged in conducting and funding research in health-related areas. His first task was to develop a Strategy for Research and Development (R&D) in health care, published in 1991 (DoH, 1991). A Central Council for Research and Development was established, chaired by the National Director. The aims of the Central Council are to:

- Identify research priorities for the NHS.
- Initiate major research programmes on these topics.

- Establish links with other research funding bodies such as the Medical Research Council, Economic and Social Research Council, charities and voluntary agencies.
- Set up structures for the dissemination of research information.
- Develop a strategy for research training and career structure.
- Charge regional R&D committees with the duty of implementing the plans of the Central Council at local level.

Clearly, all this has had great implications for nursing and in 1992 a task-force was set up by the Director of R&D and the Chief Nursing Officer to develop a Strategy for Research in Nursing, Midwifery and Health Visiting. The purpose of the taskforce was to examine the implications and opportunities for the nursing profession provided by the R&D Strategy, as well as to see that the profession was able to play a full part in the overall field of health-care research. The taskforce addressed four issues:

- Identifying research and development priorities.
- Research education and training.
- Dissemination and implementation of research findings.
- Careers in research.

The report of the taskforce was published in 1993 (DoH, 1993) and made 37 recommendations, grouped under Structure and Organisation, Research Education and Training, Funding for Research and Integrating Research and Development. The recommendations are too detailed to reproduce here, but in essence the report urged both Central and Regional R&D committees to give equal consideration to funding and implementing research and development relevant to nursing.

It also made a number of suggestions about research training for nurses, such as links and secondments of nurses at clinical level to institutions of higher education. The report made a number of recommendations to purchasers and providers concerning the integration of research findings and opportunities for research in their plans and contractual obligations. It recommended that a national nursing and midwifery research database be established.

All this will take time to work through to nurses in their everyday work situations. However, even with the re-organisation of regional health authorities which has come about since the DoH Strategy was published, there is now at both national and local level a cohesive and comprehensive research and development plan. The result of both the Strategy for Nursing Research and the original R&D Strategy has been that the importance of nursing research is being recognised at all levels. Nurses are now involved in the decision-making processes concerning research which were set up as a result of the R&D Strategy. Funds made available by the DoH for R&D are equally open to the nursing profession and plans are in hand to develop the research training and career opportunities for nurses.

FUNDING FOR RESEARCH

With the advent of the DoH R&D Strategy, the funding situation has been changed radically. Apart from the establishment of the central and regional R&D committees, the main thrust of the strategy has been to bring together, or set up links with, all the other bodies which fund research in health-related topics. These include industry, voluntary agencies, the Medical Research Council and the Economic and Social Research Council. In some cases arrangements have been made to fund large projects jointly, or at least to ensure that such bodies share the same priorities for allocation of funds. If you are looking for funding on a large scale, your first point of call should be the regional research and development manager who will be able to advise you. Such grants are, however, intended for those who already have a good track record of research and the scene is very much one of change. The best advice at present, if you are just starting out and wish to seek funding for research, is to ask the nurse adviser to the district or trust who may be able to help, or talk to a tutor or a nurse researcher known to you, who will be able to discuss the options in more detail.

Regional Health Authorities

Regional Health Authorities are the structural focus for the R&D Strategy, with an R&D director and committee in each region. As regions are due to be phased out during 1995/6 it is not clear as yet how these functions will be discharged in future. Most regions at present award scholarships or travel bursaries for nurses on an annual basis, but these are usually fairly modest in size.

LOCAL SOURCES

The new district health authorities and NHS trusts differ in their approach to funding research to be carried out by employees for the benefit of the local population.

Some may have charitable or trust funds available, but it is probably true to say that at present the structure of the NHS is changing so fast that many levels of the organisation have not developed a clear policy.

MEDICAL CHARITIES

There is a vast number of medical charities catering for specific conditions. Some are concerned more with patient support services, but most also have research commitments. While many are now putting their efforts into collaborative ventures and larger projects, they are worth trying if the research is concerned with their particular interest.

The Hospital and Health Service Year Book, which will be found in a hospital or university library, will be helpful in providing names and addresses. There are also other guides, such as:

Handbook of British Medical Charities
Directory of Grant Making Trusts
Yearbook of Grant Awarding Bodies
Royal College of Nursing Directory for Funding

CHANGES TO NURSE TRAINING AND FURTHER EDUCATION

The most fundamental change to nurse training was Project 2000, introduced in 1988. While not all schools of nursing offer this programme, more and more nurses are trained in this way for whatever branch of nursing they have chosen. The main point of Project 2000 is, of course, that nursing students are truly students, rather than the 'apprentices' which they once resembled. The difference is more than simply one of status, as the course requires nurses to think about the *why* of nursing practice, rather than only the *how*. Clearly, this means that nursing students should read the research that provides the rationale on which nursing practice is based. The other change that came about at much the same time as Project 2000 was the move of many schools of nursing into centres of higher education, such as universities and colleges, for both basic and advanced nursing studies. Furthermore, with the system of credit accumulation, whereby students build up credits for advanced nursing courses, nursing is being drawn into the mainstream of higher education. These institutions have a tradition of research as a basic principle of scholarship in all disciplines, so nursing courses have been challenged to adopt the same attitude and introduce research-based teaching and reasoning as part and parcel of the curriculum. All these developments mean that research is no longer an optional extra for a few keen souls, but something every nurse needs to understand and utilise. Not every nurse wants to carry out research for herself, but all nurses now should be able to read research with understanding and utilise the findings where it is appropriate to his or her field of practice.

Some nurses decide to pursue their interest in research even further. Although the recommendations relating to education and training in research for nurses made by the taskforce are not yet in place, courses on research methods and understanding are offered in some schools of nursing, or by the institutions for higher education to which they are now increasingly linked. It is worth talking to one of the tutors or lecturers to find out what is available locally. More and more nurses are now looking to study for university degrees, the range and organisation of which have grown enormously in recent years. It is not possible here to list all those but they fall roughly into three types.

First degree

This will lead to the award of Bachelor of Science or Bachelor of Arts. There is an increasing number of degree courses especially designed for nurses, usually for a BSc. Many build on the 'credits' gained by English National Board courses such as those in renal nursing or coronary care. Such courses will incorporate the execution of a research project as part of the requirements for the award of the degree.

Higher degree (taught)

A Master of Arts or Master of Science is the 'next level' degree. They may be called 'taught' courses because attendance at formal lectures and other settings is required. However, students are also expected to conduct a fairly major piece of research which will be supervised, but which is entirely at their own instigation and their responsibility.

Higher degree (untaught)

The degrees of Master of Philosophy and Doctor of Philosophy are awarded on the basis of original research undertaken by the student, though with supervision from a tutor and Supervisory Board. Some Universities now offer research methodology modules which the student may choose to attend, or students may arrange attendance at other relevant lectures. Clearly, this level of study is only suitable for those who have considerable research experience and probably a second professional qualification.

Nurses must learn to take advantage of these new opportunities. Does your hospital have a nursing research interest group, or a research nurse? Is there a data base of nursing research in your health district? If you don't know the answers, find out! If the answers are 'No' then perhaps you should do something about it. If nurses don't make the most of all this, we will only have ourselves to blame!

REFERENCES

Department of Health (1991) *Research for Health: A Research and Development Strategy for the NHS*. London: HMSO.
Department of Health (1993) *Report of the Taskforce on the Strategy for Research in Nursing, Midwifery and Health Visiting*. London: Department of Health.

FURTHER READING

Brittain R D (1980) Money and methods for research in the National Health Service. *Royal Society of Health Journal*, **100** (3): 79–81.

Clamp C G L with contributions from Ballard M P and Gough S (1991) *Resources for Nursing Research: an annotated bibliography*. London: ENB.

Department of Health (1993) *Research for Health*. London: Department of Health.

Institute of Nursing (1991) *Directory of Funding for Nurses*. Oxford: Institute of Nursing.

Polit D F and Hungler P B (1985) *Essentials of Nursing Research*, pp. 364–365. London: J B Lippincott.

Treece E W and Treece J W (1986) *Elements of Research in Nursing*, pp. 117–122. St Louis: Mosby.

Epilogue

We hope that now you have finished this book you will feel that it has achieved what it set out to do, which was to demonstrate that research is a 'friendly' activity. We hope also that through working through the chapters, following the scenarios and completing the exercises you have learnt to understand the research process.

In the ever-changing world of health care, an understanding of research and confidence about researching their practice is now very important for nurses and other health care professionals. As a researcher you will experience 'ups' and 'downs', as we have tried to demonstrate. There are usually some dark days in the middle of a research project when things don't go the way you hoped, but the sense of achievement when you overcome such setbacks is tremendous.

Even if you decide you do not want to actually carry out research, hopefully through this book you will be able to make the best use possible of other people's work in order to improve the care you give which, after all, is what nursing research is all about.

Glossary

Abstract Collection of published research literature which includes a summary of the work.

Action research An experiment in an everyday setting where the researcher introduces change and assesses the outcomes.

Aim Purpose for which the project was undertaken.

Approach The type of research to be conducted, i.e. survey, experimental or interpretative.

Average Statistic summarising the typical value from a set of data. Three types – mean, median and mode.

Bibliography Lists of published material, e.g. books, articles, conference papers.

Chi-squared (χ^2) Statistical test for checking relationships between variables in contingency tables (non-parametric).

Clinical audit The critical analysis of the quality of all aspects of health care.

Coding Translating responses to a survey into number codes for processing by a computer statistical package

Contingency table Table which can show the relative proportions of frequencies of two or more variables.

Continuous data (see parametric data).

Control group A group of subjects in an experiment who are observed under usual conditions to compare with the results of intervention with an experimental group.

Controlled variable A variable which is held constant during research, so that it does not interfere with changes in other variables under study.

Correlation The degree of relationship between two continuous variables expressed as a correlation coefficient between –1 and +1.

Cross-tabulation (see Contingency table).

Data Information or facts systematically gathered during research.

Data analysis techniques which summarise data to identify patterns and order.

Dependent variable   The variable which is examined for changes brought about by manipulating the independent variable.

Descriptive statistics   Techniques that help to describe patterns in the data.

Discrete data   (see non-parametric data).

Empirical   Relating to a method of testing any hypothesis by a systematically controlled collection of data.

Ethical   Relating to moral principles or value.

Evaluation research   The systematic collection of information about people, performance and products in order to improve effectiveness.

Experimental research   Research which tests an hypothesis by means of a controlled manipulation of variables.

Exploratory research   An early stage in some research projects using informal observation and interview methods to refine the hypotheses and research design.

Frequency table   A table that shows how frequently certain categories of data occur.

Graph   The visual display of data on a chart, e.g. histogram.

Historical research   Research which collects and interprets evidence on past events, sometimes indicating their implications for the future.

Hypothesis   Statement which predicts the relationship between variables in a study

Independent variable   The variable that is manipulated during the research.

Index   Lists of published research articles and papers, often covering foreign language sources as well as English-speaking ones.

Inferential statistics   Statistical tests which help to make inferences from data, such as causal relationships between variables.

Interpretative research   Research that seeks to understand the question under study from the perspective of those participating in the setting.

Main study   The major enterprise of the research project, conducted after the pilot study.

Mean   A statistic to average data by summing the values of all observations and dividing by the number of observations.

Median   An average that identifies the value that is exactly half way in the order of values in the data.

Methodology   The methods by which data is collected, e.g. interview, observation. In a wider sense it also means the study of the methods themselves.

Mode   A way of averaging data by expressing the value that occurs most often.

Non-parametric data   Measures in discrete categories and not in numerical order, e.g. different professions, days of the week.

Non-participant observation   A data collection method in which the researcher takes no active part in the situation being observed.

Normal distribution Smooth, symmetrical 'bell-shaped' curve in a plot of frequency measures. Necessary if statistical tests are to be applied to the data.

Null hypothesis Statement which predicts no relationship between variables being tested. Basic principle of statistical tests. If tests reject null hypothesis, this suggests that a relationship does exist.

Nursing research Research concerned with issues of nursing practice, management or education.

Observation A method of collecting data by one or more researchers watching and systematically recording the actions or behaviour of those being studied.

Official statistics The 'book-keeping' data of various government departments pulbished for general use.

Parametric Relating to rules or parameters which data must conform to in the use of certain statistical tests.

Parametric data Measures on a continuous scale, e.g. salary, temperature.

Participant observation A method in which the researcher is actively engaged in the situation being observed.

Percentage Data standardised to show incidence per hundred cases.

Pilot study A small preparatory study usually conducted to test data collection methods

Population The total number of people or things in a particular category of interest for study.

Probability The principle behind statistical procedures which help to assess whether the results of a study show a pattern or occur by chance only.

Project An activity which seeks to provide information, and which may or may not be empirically based.

Qualitative research Research in which the data is in the form of words, and the analysis aims at identifying underlying concepts and commonly held themes.

Quantitative research Research in which the data collected is in the form of numbers, and which seeks to test the hypothesis by statistical analysis of data.

Quasi-experiment An experiment conducted in an everyday setting which therefore does not fully conform to the strict rules of a laboratory study.

Questionnaire A written list of questions which is put to respondents on attitudes, opinions or experiences. They may be administered by the respondent, or by the researcher.

Random sample A sample chosen so that all members of the population have an equal chance of being represented to eliminate bias.

Reactivity Influence of the researcher on the research setting and the data collected.

Regression analysis An advanced statistical procedure concerned with the nature of the relationship between continuous variables.

Reliability The extent to which research findings can be generalised to other settings. Can relate to time and place.

Replication The repeat of previously published research, following the original research design as closely as possible.

Research critique The critical examination of published research.

Research project A study conforming to scientific principles, and contributing to the body of knowledge of the discipline.

Research proposal A paper, sometimes formal in structure, which sets out the research question to be examined, the intended design of the study, and the expected benefits of the research.

Respondent The person under study in a survey.

Response rate Proportion of respondents invited to participate in a study who eventually provide data.

Sample A sub-set of the population, chosen according to statistical procedures, on which data will be collected.

Scatter plot Data from two continuous variables plotted in relation to each other on the two axes of a graph.

Semi-structured interview An interview where the questions to some topics are open-ended and some are structured or closed.

Standard deviation A measure of the variability represented in a normal distribution of data, showing by how much the scores deviate from the mean.

Statistics This can mean the data itself, the activity of analysing the data, or specific statistical tests.

Statistical significance Where statistical tests show that results were probably not achieved by chance factors, e.g. 'significance level $p < 0.01$' means that the probability of results occuring by chance is no more than once in a hundred.

Stratified sample A sample chosen to represent specific categories in the population.

Structured interview A carefully controlled interview in which a set pattern of questions is put to a respondent.

Survey research Research which seeks to describe and analyse the present situation by means of questionnaires, tests or interviews with a sample of the population.

Table The representation of data in orderly columns for easier reference.

Theory A structure which sets out in a formal manner the inter-relatedness of concepts in a particular field of scholarship.

Triangulation The use of more than one approach, methodology or theoretical framework in a single research enterprise.

Unstructured interview An interview in which topics pertinent to the research are posed in such a way as to allow the respondent free expression.

Validity   The ability of a data collecting method or instrument to measure what it is supposed to measure.

Variable   Any characteristic, quality or attribute which varies, can be observed and can be measured.

Index

Page numbers in italics refer to definitions in the Glossary

abstracts 19, 23, 27, *181*
accident reports 45–6
acknowledgements, in reports 154
action research 65, *181*
    v. evaluation research 64
advisers (mentors) 9, 160–1
aim 7, *181*
American Journal of Nursing Company International Nursing Index 23
analysis, *see* data analysis
anonymity, of questionnaires 79
approach (type of research) 43–8, *181*
attitude scales 85
audit
    clinical 169, *181*
    of clinical practice 168
    cycle of 169–70
    definitions 168–9
    design 172
    differences from research 170–1
    of medical practice 168
    relationship with research 169–72
    research's part in 2
    role of research in 169–70
    stages in 169–70
averages 123–4, *181*
    see also mean; median; mode
awareness files and boards 30

bar charts 122
bias, in sampling 88
bibliographies 19, 23, *181*
brainstorming 7–8, 13–14

cafeteria questions, *see* multiple-choice questions
cameras, hidden 109–10
case histories 45, 107–8
CD-ROM 20
censuses 118
Central Council for Research and Development 174–5
Central Statistical Office (CSO) publications 119
charities, medical 176–7
check-list questions, *see* multiple-choice questions
chi-squared test 129–31, *181*
CINAHL (Cumulative Index of Nursing and Allied Health) 20
clinical audit 169, *181*
cluster sampling 89
coding *181*
    of questionnaire answers 91–6
coding frames 94, 96
coding sheets 91, 93
Collaborative Evaluation model 66
colleagues, information for 150
community care survey (example)
    consent form 100
    data collection forms 97, 98–9
    hypotheses 97
    interview schedules 100–1, 102
Compact Disc Read Only Memory (CD-ROM) 20
complaints reports 46
computer modelling 47
computers
    advice on analysis by 94, 96

coding questionnaires for 91–6
data analysis by 133
literature searching 20–1
conclusions
  critical evaluation of 28–9
  from research project 153
confidentiality
  of questionnaires 79
  right to 143
consent
  ethical 147
  exercises 147–8
  to interview 104
  obligation to obtain 144–5
  right to refuse 143
  sample form 100
  services not dependent on 143
  vulnerable groups 143–4
content analysis
  of documents 45
  of questionnaires 94, 95
contingency tables (cross-tabulation)
    127–9, *181*
continuous data, *see* parametric
    data
control groups 36, 60, 61–2, *181*
controlled variable *181*
correlation 132, *181*
costing, of research project 161, 164
critical incident techniques 46
critique, research *184*
  example 36–7
  exercise 37
  study evaluated 31–5
  see also evaluation
cross-tabulation (contingency tables)
    127–9, *181*
Cumulative Index of Nursing and
    Allied Health (CINAHL) 20

data *181*
  continuous (parametric) 124, 133,
    183
  discrete (non-parametric) 124, 133,
    182
data analysis *181*
  deviant cases 113
  evaluation of 28–9
  exercises 133–6, 137
  multiple variables 126–33
  qualitative data 111–13
  quantitative data 117
  single variable 119–26

worked examples 120–30
  see also statistics
data recording
  ideas gained during research 111
  observation notes 110–11
decision-driven research 40
degree courses 177–8
Delphi system 46
Department of Health
  abstracts 23
  library 23
dependent variables 55, 62, *182*
depth interviews 108
descriptive research, *see* survey
    research
descriptive statistics *182*
descriptive theory 42
design, of research study
  anticipating confidentiality problems
    143
  choice of method 39–41
  fit of theory and method 41–3
  ideas from literature search 17
  triangulation 50, *184*
dignity, right to 143
Directory of Grant Making Trusts 177
discrete data, *see* non-parametric data
District Health Authorities
  and research funding 176
documents
  content analysis 45
  as data source 45

Economic and Social Research
    Council, and research funding 176
education and training
  changes in 1, 177
  degree courses 177–8
  DoH Strategy recommendation 175
  English National Board courses 178
  higher 177
  Project 200 177
  reason for research proposal 158
  research-based 177
  in research methods and under-
    standing 177
empirical, definition *182*
ENB (English National Board)
    courses 178
encyclopaedias 20
English National Board (ENB)
    courses 178
ethical, definition *182*

ethical committees
formal protocol document 145–7
membership of 145
role of 144, 145
timing of applications to 146–7
ethics
considerations in research proposals 159
definition 141
evaluating research 28, 29
examples of ethical consent needed 147
and experimental methods 62–3
and observation techniques 109–10
RCN guidelines for research 144
rights of the individual 142–3
vulnerable groups 143–4
evaluation formative 65
evaluation, of published research
check-list of questions 29
key questions 26–9
terminology problems 30
see also critique
evaluation research
v. action research 64
definition 63–4, 182
exercises 66–8
experimental design in 63
feedback cycle 64
models of 64–5, 66
process of 64–5
experience, as source of research problem 8–9
experimental research 43, 48, 54
before-and-after design 59–60
definitions 55–6, 182
ethical considerations 62–3
exercises 58–61
quasi-experiments 62
see also action research;
evaluation research; hypothesis;
variables
experts, obtaining opinions from 46
explanatory theory 42
exploratory research 47, 52, 182

feedback
for colleagues 150
in evaluation cycle 64
for funding bodies 149
for participants 150
field notes 111

Flanagan's Critical Incident Technique 46
focused interviews 106–7
frequency tables 120–1, 182
chi-squared test 129–31, 181
funding
application for 158, 160
guidelines for proposals 160
medical charities 176–7, 179
reporting to funding bodies 149
request for further funds 149
sources 176–7
'fuzzies' and 'non-fuzzies', statements and words 11–12

game simulation 47
government statistics, see official statistics
graded alternative questions 84
graphs 121, 182
scatter plots 129, 130, 184
grounded theory 43, 113
Guide to Official Statistics 119
Guttman scale 85

Handbook of British Medical Charities 176
harm, and individual rights 142
Hawthorne effect 109
Health Information Service 19
Health Service Abstracts (DoH) 23
historical research 44, 182
Hospital and Health Service Yearbook 176, 179
hypothesis 56–7, 182
null 56, 183

incident reports 46
independent variables 55, 62, 182
Index Medicus 23
indexes 19–20, 23, 182
inferential statistics 131–3, 182
International Nursing Index 23
interpretative research 44, 48, 182
interviewers, reactivity to 49–50
interviewing, skills of 90
interviews
advantages and disadvantages 71
case histories 107–8
data analysis 112–13
depth 108
focused (guided) 106–7

life histories 107–8
  problems with 107
  sample schedules 101–2
  semi-structured 74, 106, *184*
  setting up 104
  structured 73, 105–6, *184*
  transcribing data 112
  types of 105
  unstructured *184–5*
  use of tape-recorders 106–7
  see also questionnaires; surveys

Journal Clubs 30
journals
  publication of research papers
    155–6
  see also literature

Kardex files 22
key words 18–19
King's Fund Library 22
knowledge, nursing, types of 39
knowledge-driven research 40

lateral thinking 7
libraries 18–19, 22–3
life histories 45, 107–8
Likert scale 85
literature
  awareness of 30
  finding research ideas from 9
  research/non-research 18
  see also critique; evaluation;
    journals; references
literature reviews
  in evaluating research 27, 29
  in research proposals 160, 163
  in written reports 152
literature search
  computer searching 20–1
  continuous process 16
  critical reading of research 26–8
  directed 16–17
  information sources 18–21, 22–3
  key words in 18–19
  preliminary 16
  proportion of time spent on 16
  purposes 17–18
  recording relevant references 22
  relevant authors 19
  'snowball' method 20–1
  types of literature 18
local taxation records 118

main study 76, *182*
Mann-Whitney *U* test 133
Matched Pairs *t*-test 133
mean 123, *182*
median 123, 123–4, *182*
medical charities 176–7
Medical Research Council 176
Medline 20
mentors 9, 160–1
methodology *182*
  explained in research report 152–3
microfiche 19
Minitab 133
mirrors, one-way 47, 109–10, 110
mode 123, 124, *182*
multiple-choice questions 77, 82–3, 84

National Health Service (NHS),
    research and development in
    174–6
NHS Trusts, and research funding 176
non-parametric (discrete) data *182*
non-participant observation
  closed 109–10
  definition 109, *182*
  open 109
normal distribution 125–6, *183*
null hypothesis 56, *183*
nurses
  need for knowledge of research 3
  need to question practice 7
  reasons for not using research
    findings 2
  research opportunities for 178
  as researchers 7
nursing
  definition 39
  gap between knowledge and
    practice 2
  professionalism in 1
  as research-based profession 2
  theory, *see* theory
  types of knowledge
  see also education and training
Nursing Index 23
nursing research *183*
  see also research
Nursing Research Abstracts (DoH) 23

observation *183*
  data analysis 112–13
  example of 113–14
  exercises on 114–15

non-participant 109–10, *182*
participant 110, *183*
recording data 110–11
roles of the observer 108–9, 110
of situations 108–10
of specific events 108
official statistics 118–19, *183*
one-way mirrors 47, 109–10, 110

parametric, definition *183*
parametric (continuous) data 124, 133, *183*
participant observation 110, *183*
participants, information for 150
participation, right of refusal 143
Pearson, Product–Moment Correlation 132
percentage 120, *183*
pie charts 122
pilot studies 75, *183*
and research evaluation 29
population 87–8, *183*
Population Trends 119
practitioners, as researchers 7
predictive theory 42
privacy, right to 143
probability *183*
probability methods of sampling 88
probability statistics, *see* inferential statistics
problem-solving model 3, 7
problems, for research, *see* topics
professionalism in nursing 1
Project 2000 177
projects *183*
finding ideas for 7–11
research project *184*
proposals, research *184*
construction of 159
contents 161–4
coverage of 158, 160
ethical considerations 159
example of 164–6
guidelines from funding bodies 160
methodological considerations 159
objectives of study 163
political considerations 159
purposes of 158
stages in preparation 160–1
style of 160
publication, writing for 155–6

reluctance to publish 156

qualitative research 39, 40, 41, 43, 48 *183*
data analysis 111–13
v. quantitative, example 50–1
see also interviews; observation
quality considerations 172
quantitative research 39, 40, 40–1, 43, 47, *183*
v. qualitative, example 50–1
see also questionnaires
quasi-experiments 62, *183*
questionnaires *183*
bad, example of 86–7
coding 91–6
confidentiality and anonymity 79
covering letter 79, 80
design 76–9
instructions on 76–7
introductory paragraph 78–9
language of 76
postal 71
respondents' comments 77
response rates 90–1
self-completion 71
semi-structured 106
sequence of questions in 77–8
standardised, structured 105–6
structured, *see* structured question-naires
see also interviews; questions; surveys
questions
attitude scales 85
branching 78
closed 72, 85
coding of answers to 91–6
easily understandable 76
graded alternatives 84
instructions for answering 76–7
multiple-choice 77, 82–3, 84
open 71, 73, 74, 82, 85
overlapping categories in 85
rank-ordering 83
types of 82
wording of 79–82
yes/no 77, 82
quota sampling 89–90

random sample 88, *183*
rank-ordering questions 83
reactivity 49–50, *183*

reading, as source of research problem 9

recommendations
  evaluation of 29
  in written reports 153

records, *see* data recording; documents; literature

references
  cataloguing 22
  recording information from 22
  in research studies 27, 29
  systems of quoting 22
  in written reports 155
  see also literature search

Regional Health Authorities 176

registers of research 19–20

registration statistics 118

regression analysis 132, *184*

reliability 49, *184*

Repertory Grid 85

replication, of previous research 21, *184*

reports
  appropriate to recipient 150
  contents of 151–5
  exercises 157
  for funding bodies 149
  information to be conveyed in 150–1
  for publication 155–6
  stages in writing 151
  visual appearance of 153–4
  see also feedback

research
  aim of 7, *181*
  approach-method relationships in 48
  choice of topic for 9–11
  classification 144
  critique, *see* critique, research
  a cyclic process 4–5
  definition 3
  methods of 39–41, 43–8
  projects, *see* projects
  proposals, *see* proposals, research
  reasons for not using findings 2
  a scientific approach 3
  sources of problems for 8–9
  statements, *see* statements, research
  steps in 3, 4
  theoretical (basic) *v.* practical (applied) 40
  use of knowledge of 1–2
  see also research study

Research and Development Strategy 2–3

research study
  critique of 36–7
  ethical issues in 28
  example of 31–5

researchers, practitioners as 7

respondents 105, 107, *184*

response rates 90–41, *184*

results, of research
  communication of 149
  evaluation of 28–9
  see also conclusions; feedback; recommendations; reports

review of literature, *see* literature search

rights of the individual 142–3

Royal College of Nursing
  Bibliography 23
  Directory for Funding 177
  guidelines on ethics of research 144
  Library 22
  research adviser 161

sample/sampling
  bias in 88
  cluster 89
  definitions 87–8, *184*
  methods of sampling 88–90
  probability methods 88
  quota 89–90
  random 88, *183*
  rules in sampling 88
  simple 88
  size of sample 90
  stratified 89, *184*
  worked example 88–90

scatter plots 129, 130, *184*

Scottish Health Service Library 23

self-determination, right to 142

self-respect, right to 143

Semantic Differential technique 85

semi-structured interviews *184*

significance, statistical 131–2, *184*

Social Trends 119

Spearman Rank Order Correlation 132

SPSS (Statistical Package for the Social Sciences) 133

stake-holders 66

standard deviation 124–6, *184*
standards, and audit 169–70
statements, research
  'fuzzy' 11–12
  generation of hypotheses from 56–7
  key words 18–19
  as questions 12, 13
  refining 11–13
Statistical Package for the Social
  Sciences (SPSS) 133
statistical significance 131–2, *184*
statistical tests, evaluation of 28
statistics
  in data analysis 119
  definitions 117–18, *184*
  descriptive *182*
  inferential (probability) 131–3,
    182
  official 118–19, *183*
  techniques and worked examples
    119–32
  see also computers; data analysis;
    graphs; tables
Strategy for Research and
  Development 175, 176
Strategy for Research in Nursing,
  Midwifery and Health Visiting
  175–6
stratified sample 89, *184*
structured interviews *184*
structured questionnaires 72–4, *184*
  exploratory stage 75
  main study 76, *182*
  pilot study 75, *183*
survey research 44, 48, *184*
surveys
  definition 70–1
  exercise 96
  official 118
  styles of 71
  see also interviews; questionnaires;
    structured questionnaires

t-test 133
tables *184*
  contingency (cross-tabulation)
    127–9, *181*
  frequency tables 120–1, *182*

  of multiple variables 126–9
  of single variables 120–1
tape recorders 106–7
terminology 27–8, 30
theory *184*
  deductive 41–2
  descriptive 42
  explanatory 42
  grounded 43, 113
  inductive 41–2
  and literature search 17
  predictive 42
  research based on 39–40, 41–3
  as source of research problem 9
Thurstone scale 85
topics, for research
  choice of 8–11
  see also statements, research
training, *see* education and training
transcripts 112
triangulation 50, *184*

unstructured interviews *184–5*

validity *185*
  external 49
  internal 49
  structured surveys 74
variables
  causality rules 61
  confounding (extraneous,
    uncontrolled) 61, 67
  control of 57–61
  controlled *181*
  defining 17
  definition 55, *185*
  dependent 55, 62, *182*
  independent 55, 62, *182*

Wilcoxon Matched Pairs Signed Rank
  Test 133
words/deeds dilemma 75
Working for Patients (White Paper)
  168

Yearbook of Grant Awarding Bodies
  177
yes/no questions 77, 82